MANAGEME

of

CELIAC DISEASE

BY

SIDNEY VALENTINE HAAS, M.D.

Professor of Pediatrics and Director of the Department, New York Polyclinic Medical School and Hospital; Consultant, Lebanon Hospital, Harlem Hospital, and Riverside Hospital for Contagious Diseases of the New York Health Department; Fellow of the New York Academy of Medicine

AND

MERRILL PATTERSON HAAS, M.D.

12 Illustrations

Preface

Years of clinical experience during which we have seen and treated hundreds of cases of celiac disease have led us to evolve a treatment for this illness which has been shown to be effective. Years of careful thought and experiment have led us, too, to evolve an etiologic hypothesis which may point the way to further research to the end that medical science may ultimately solve the riddle of celiac disease. Our work has been based not only upon our clinical experience but also upon the work of hundreds of other scientists who have helped to cast light upon the causes and the treatment of this disease. This monograph is an attempt to report not only our own experiences and ideas but also those of others who have tackled the problem.

We have divided the monograph into two basic parts. In the first, we discuss the various aspects of celiac disease as they have been treated by other investigators. In the second, "Celiac Disease Today," we have confined ourselves to our own ideas on the subject. This division, we feel, will make the monograph most helpful, both to the student of celiac disease and to the busy practitioner.

The bibliography, which was prepared by Milton L. Zisowitz, is, we believe, the most nearly complete that has ever been assembled on the subject of celiac disease. We feel that it will be of great value to all who desire to pursue further studies.

The illustrations selected for inclusion in the text represent two cases treated thirty years ago when the present treatment was new, two cases in which the cure has been completed recently and one case in process of treatment at the present time.

The table of symptoms (chiefly avitaminosis) was compiled from the first group of cases published in 1924, but not included in the paper because of lack of space.

Although we accept full responsibility for both the virtues and the defects which may appear in the following pages, we should like to acknowledge our indebtedness to those who helped us in our task. We owe a debt of thanks to various medical librarians, especially those of the New York Academy of Medicine Library, of the Library of the American Medical Association, of the Army Medical Library, and particularly to Mrs. Lilian E. Nugent, librarian of the Queens County Medical Society Library. We should also like to express our deep appreciation to Marshall McClintock and to Milton L. Zisowitz who assisted us in the preparation of the manuscript.

S.V.H.
M.P.H.

Contents

MANAGEMENT OF
CELIAC DISEASE

ORIENTATION

The authors believe that the work presents, for the first time, in permanent form, the summation of many years of research and experience in celiac disease.

The clinical findings are based upon 603 cases of celiac disease treated by diet. This study presents the results in the 370 cases treated long enough to arrive at conclusions.

Celiac disease is defined as a protracted intermittent diarrhea which results from the ingestion of carbohydrates other than those in fruits, some vegetables and protein milk. The disease may occur at any time after birth but starts most commonly between the ages of six and twelve months. Early recognition is important.

Only in advanced cases of celiac disease does one find such classical symptoms as protruding abdomen and extreme emaciation. Milder cases show: (1) diarrhea with mushy, voluminous, foul stools; (2) irritability; (3) anorexia; (4) failure to gain weight; (5) sometimes colic and vomiting.

Diagnosis depends on the clinical picture, the case history and the response to the specific carbohydrate diet described.

This diet differs from other "celiac diets" in excluding *all* carbohydrates except those in fruits, some vegetables and protein milk. It permits fat in normal amounts.

The basic components of this diet are bananas, protein milk, meat and cheese. Later, other fruits, eggs and some vegetables are added. Supplements of vitamins and iron are recommended.

This diet is strictly maintained for *at least* 12 months, then cereals, potatoes and sugars may be tried, one at a time. After 3 months plain milk is added. If the milk is tolerated, cure may be considered complete.

Prognosis of celiac disease is excellent. There is complete recovery with no relapses, no deaths, no crises, no pulmonary involvement and no stunting of growth.

This specific carbohydrate diet is a good diagnostic tool and a uniformly successful treatment for celiac disease.

1

Scope and Purpose of the Work

Three factors have long served to confuse the investigation, the discussion and the treatment of celiac disease. First, its etiology remains unknown despite repeated assaults from many directions aimed at revealing this well-hidden secret. Second, its symptoms are found in so many conditions and are subject to so many variations that recognition of their true significance is often difficult. Third, no simple and clear-cut diagnostic test or procedure has been developed. As a result, many cases of celiac disease, especially those of a mild nature, go unrecognized, and some patients are treated as celiacs when actually they do not suffer from that ailment. The quick cures no doubt fall in the latter category.

This threefold confusion is further confounded by a confusion of tongues, by a multiplicity of terms and names. The disease has been called Gee's disease, Gee-Herter disease, Herter-Heubner disease, infantilism, intestinal infantilism, starch intolerance, fat intolerance, idiopathic steatorrhea, nontropical sprue, severe chronic digestive insufficiency of children past infancy (Heubner), acholia (Cheadle), chronic intestinal indigestion, pancreatic insufficiency, hepatic insufficiency, chronic recurrent diarrhea, atrophia pluriglandularis (Schick and Wagner) and identical with sprue. Recently, in many circles, it has lost the dignity of being called a disease and is referred to only as a syndrome behind which none, one, or several diseases hide themselves. At one time or another it has been considered a bacterial infection, a disturbance of the nervous system, an allergy, avitaminosis, cystic fibrosis, hypothyroidism, a faulty fat metabolism and absorption, an endocrine disturbance and a general constitutional weakness.

In this work we speak of celiac disease deliberately as a disease because it is a condition of abnormal physiology with a characteristic syndrome, the symptoms of which respond favorably to a definite mode of therapy. Many workers in the field agree with the definition of celiac disease which we present here, but we shall not limit our inquiry to that concept only. On the contrary, we shall try to present fully every view of this condition, every current theory as to its etiology, and the various modes of therapy in use today, together with supporting evidence gathered by the many investigators.

In this effort to organize and synthesize the reported work on celiac disease and related conditions, we have come to the encouraging conclusion that, despite the apparent multiplicity of names, theories and treatments, there is actually a very large area of agreement. So little evidence has been produced to substantiate any theory of etiology that one can scarcely say that there is disagreement in this field; there is, rather, ignorance and a tentative suggestion of one cause or another that may eventually be discovered. There is some disagreement as to the breadth or narrowness of the term, celiac disease; for example, most contemporary writers feel that cystic fibrosis of the pancreas is a separate disease entity, although it presents the same symptoms as celiac disease, but there is the possibility that it is merely another and more severe form of celiac disease. But since there is unanimous recognition of both conditions, the disagreement is little more than one of terminology, which will be settled when etiologic secrets are unearthed.

The wide variety of treatments recommended twenty years

ago has been reduced to a generally accepted method of therapy—by diets, with differences only in details. The chief disagreement concerns the role of fats in the diet, and there are some differences as to which carbohydrates must be excluded and which are permissible. Although superficially these differences of opinion may seem trivial, unfortunately they have an important bearing on prognosis. Some workers stress more than others the importance of supplementary medications, such as liver extracts, pancreatin, or antibiotics. The difference here, however, is one of emphasis rather than of basic approach to the problem.

Disagreements are likely to loom larger than agreements. As a result, there has been a feeling that wide gulfs separate the chief investigators of celiac disease. An examination of all the views reveals, however, that there are only different angles of vision. We hope that by gathering together in this work all the points of view, a more nearly complete picture with better perspective may be presented.

We shall present, first, a historical review of published work on celiac disease and related conditions from the earliest known publications up to the time of writing. This will be followed by a section on the clinical and pathologic symptoms of the disease, together with opinions as to its incidence. The many theories as to etiology will be outlined. Much important laboratory work has been done on the chemical and anatomic pathology of celiac disease, especially in the past twenty years, and a summary of this work in many fields will be given. As a result, we shall be able to arrive at a meaningful definition of celiac disease, or at least a general definition with qualifications offered by some contemporary physicians. Methods of diagnosis and treatment will be reviewed, together with opinions as to prognosis. In the final section of this work we shall present our point of view concerning celiac disease—a point of view based on more than 30 years of clinical experience with more than 600 cases, coupled with a careful study of the literature.

Many basic facts about celiac disease are still unknown. A review of the literature on the subject shows that widespread interest in the condition has developed only in the last quarter century. In the 35 years between Gee's report in 1888 and the first paper on the value of the banana in 1923, approximately 100 papers on the ailment were published. Since that time, some 450 papers have appeared. Up to 1923 there were only some 30 American papers, while about 125 have been printed since that date. There are still many promising lines of inquiry open, as we hope to show in our final chapter. Finally, the bibliography on the subject presented at the end of this work is, we believe, the most exhaustive ever assembled. It should prove of value to everyone interested in celiac disease.

2

History

A careful examination of medical literature reveals that apparently celiac disease has always existed. The similarity of its symptoms to those of several other conditions and the lack of any obvious cause long prevented its recognition as a distinct ailment. Since there exists even today disagreement over terminology and the precise nature of celiac disease, it is not extraordinary that only very few men recognized, before the turn of the century, that a confusing combination of more or less common symptoms constituted a definite disease.

One of the earliest references to celiac disease occurs in the work of Aretaeus the Cappadocian,[22]* "On the Causes and Symptoms of Chronic Diseases," dating probably from the time of the Roman emperor Domitian:

The stomach being the digestive organ, labors in digestion when diarrhea seizes the patient. Diarrhea consists in the discharge of undigested food in a fluid state; and if this does not proceed from a slight cause of only one or two days' duration; and if, in addition, the patient's general system be debilitated by atrophy of the body, the Coeliac disease of a chronic nature is formed, from atony of the heat which digests, and a refrigeration of the stomach, when the food, indeed, is dissolved in the heat, but the heat does not digest it, nor convert it into its proper chyme, but leaves its work half finished, from inability to complete it; the food then being deprived of this operation, is changed to a state which is bad in color, smell, and consistence. For its color is white and without bile; it has an offensive smell and is flatulent; it is liquid and wants consistence from not being completely elaborated, and from no part of the digestive process having been properly done except the commencement.

---

* Superior figures refer to the bibliography on page 155.

Wherefore they have flatulence of the stomach, continued eructations, of a bad smell; but if these pass downwards, the bowels rumble, evacuations are flatulent, thick, fluid, or clayey, along with the phantasy, as if a fluid were passing through them; heavy pain of the stomach now and then, as if from a puncture; the patient emaciated and atrophied, pale, feeble, incapable of performing any of his accustomed works.

Following this vivid, although incomplete description of clinical symptoms, Aretaeus proceeded to recommend a shotgun treatment with fasting, emetics and potions to re-kindle the heat of the stomach. One suggestion is interesting in view of the present use of banana in celiac diets— he recommends "the juice of the plantain," a prominent member of the banana family.

Medical historians have found few other references to celiac disease, under any name, in the next 16 centuries. Caelius Aurelianus [92] wrote about the condition around the fifth century. Brüning,[88] in a paper published in 1921, cited the case of one Christian Heinrich Heineken of Lübeck, who died of the disease in 1725. In 1833 Richard Bright [81] published a paper in the *Medico-Chirurgical Transactions*, describing the frequent fatty stools in several cases suffering, he believed, from some disease of the pancreas and the duodenum. William Gull,[281] writing in *Guy's Hospital Reports* in 1855, outlined the symptoms found in a 13-year-old boy that clearly suggest celiac disease as we understand it today—enlarged abdomen, frequent and voluminous stools of a dull, chalky color. In writing of the different types of fatty stools, Gull commented that "modern authors have passed over the subject or treated it lightly."

The beginning of present-day interest in celiac disease came with Samuel Gee's [205] classic report "On the Celiac Affection," published in 1888, although it was more than 30 years before much more than sporadic attention was paid to the condition. For a time each new investigator felt that he had discovered a new disease, and almost every one gave it a new name. Even though Gee's paper had little immediate influence, it has kept its pre-eminent place in celiac literature because of its thorough and vivid description of the severe celiac case and because of Gee's perception of some important facts that have stood the tests of time and investigation. Gee wrote:

There is a kind of chronic indigestion which is met with in persons of all ages, yet is especially apt to affect children between one and five years old. Signs of the disease are yielded by the faeces; being loose, not formed, but not watery; more bulky than the food taken would seem to account for; pale in colour, as if devoid of bile; yeasty, frothy, an appearance due to fermentation; stinking, stench often very great, the food having undergone putrefaction rather than concoction.

The causes of the disease are obscure. Children who suffer from it are not all weak in constitution. Errors in diet may perhaps be a cause, but what error? Why, out of a family of children all brought up in much the same way, should one alone suffer? This often happens.

Naked-eye examination of dead bodies throws no light upon the nature of the coeliac affection: nothing unnatural can be seen in the stomach, intestines, or other digestive organs.

The onset is usually gradual, so that its time is hard to fix: sometimes the complaint sets in suddenly, like an accidental diarrhea; but even when this is so, the nature of the disease soon shows itself.

The patient wastes more in the limbs than in the face, which often remains plump until death is nigh. In the limbs emaciation is at first more apparent to hand than to eye, the flesh feeling soft and flabby. Muscular weakness great; muscular tenderness often present. . . . The belly is mostly soft, doughy, and inelastic; sometimes distended and rather tight. Wind may be troublesome and very foetid. Appetite for food differs in different cases, being good, or ravenous, or bad.

The course of the disease is always slow, whatever its end; whether the patient live or die, he lingers ill for months or years. Death is a common end, and is mostly brought about by some intercurrent disorder. . . . Recovery is complete or incomplete. When recovery tends to be complete, a prevailing weakness of the legs is left long after all other tokens of the disease have passed away, a weakness which shows itself in that the child is unable to jump. When recovery is incomplete, the illness drags on for years; the patient getting better on the whole, but being very subject to relapses of his complaint. While the disease is active, the children cease to grow; even when it tends slowly to recovery, they are left frail and stunted.

(

Despite the meagerness of Gee's information about celiac disease, he saw clearly several important facts that escaped many later investigators—that "if the patient can be cured at all, it must be by means of diet," that cow's milk "is the least suited kind of food," that "highly starchy food, rice, sago, corn-flour, are unfit." He was puzzled, like so many others after him, by the failure of celiac disease to respond to the same logic that had been applied successfully to other digestive disturbances. "The disease being a failure of digestion, nothing seems more reasonable, at first sight, than to digest the patient's food artificially before it is given; but my experience has shown that peptonized milk and gruel are of little or no use in the treatment of the coeliac affection." Gee pointed out another fact of significance which is the basis of promising research today, 62 years after he wrote. "We must never forget that what the patient takes beyond his power of digestion does harm," he wrote, suggesting that unfit foods played more than a negative role and actually produced a pathologic condition in the digestive tract. Some concrete suggestions for research along this line are presented in our final chapter.

Despite Gee's keen perception in his pioneering work, his suggestions about dietary therapy were not productive of good results. Later work proved them to be unsound, although no more so than many other treatments recommended half a century after the publication of his paper.

Gee's work aroused little interest at the time. Indeed, for some years many men working in the same field seemed to be unaware of his report. But there were independent studies of celiac disease, whether called by that name or not. In 1889 R. A. Gibbons [210] suggested that the condition arose from a functional derangement of the nervous mechanism controlling the digestive glands, resulting in abnormal or insufficient secretion of digestive juices. Later studies indicated that digestive juices were normal in celiac disease, but Gibbons' suggestion of the nervous system as the originator of the condition never has received the thorough investigation that it deserved.

In 1902 Bramwell [72] reported on a case of infantilism, which he elaborated in several papers during the next few years. Apparently he was unfamiliar with the work of Gee and Gibbon and felt that he had discovered a completely new disease. His patient was a boy almost 19 years old who showed the physical development of one about 11 or 12. The symptoms, as described by Bramwell, were obviously those of celiac disease, and he carefully excluded the presence of syphilis, tuberculosis, or other possible causes. He also reported a deficiency in the pancreatic secretion and improvement upon the administration of pancreatic extract. In view of the serious investigation of the role of the pancreas in conditions displaying the celiac syndrome during the past decade, Bramwell's reports assume great historical significance.

Cheadle [104] added to the growing list of names for celiac disease in "A Clinical Lecture on Acholia," published in 1903. Referring to the work of Gee and Gibbons, he attributed the colorless stools of the condition to an absence of bile. His description was typical of the stools in celiac disease—"like a mass of white paint or white paste . . . greasy in appearance, glistening, fatty . . . distinctly offensive—often horribly so—stinking . . . larger than normal, more voluminous, as if food taken in was imperfectly absorbed." He spoke vividly of the weakness, the emaciation, the enlarged abdomen of the celiac sufferer. Although Cheadle favored Gibbons' view that the origin of the disease lay in the nervous system, he believed that the immediate cause of the symptoms was due to some dysfunction of the liver and possibly of the pancreas, despite the fact that postmortem examination revealed no lesion of those organs. Many later tests by other workers proved that biliary secretions were normal in celiac disease.

The first work that seems to have suggested bacteria as

a factor in celiac disease came from Schütz [587] in 1904. Reporting on a case with so many similarities to celiac disease that it reasonably may be assumed to have been an example of that condition, he found in the stool an abnormally large amount of fermentative and putrefactive bacteria. The normal intestine, Schütz felt, regulated the growth of bacteria, but in such cases as the one he reported, some intestinal abnormality prevented such regulation. He later agreed with other investigators that the abnormality probably was some kind of constitutional defect or weakness.

While this sporadic and inconclusive work was being done in Europe, there was even less interest in the United States. Shortly after the turn of the century, however, L. Emmett Holt, Sr., became interested in celiac disease. The tragic cases of children who slowly wasted away to death, despite all efforts to treat them, excited his sympathy and his conviction that, with sufficient study, something could be done for them. He aroused the interest of a colleague, Christian Herter,[258] then Professor of Therapeutics and Pharmacology at Columbia, who, over a period of 7 years, went deeply into the laboratory phase of the subject and, with Holt's assistance, into the clinical phases as well. His conclusions, published in 1908 in an important monograph, "On Infantilism from Chronic Intestinal Infection," follow.

In view of the many details which it has been necessary to incorporate in this study of infantilism, it seems to me desirable to summarize the chief conclusions which may be drawn.

The following are the facts which I would especially emphasize:

1. There is a pathological state of childhood marked by a striking retardation in growth of the skeleton, the muscles and the various organs and associated with a chronic intestinal infection characterized by the overgrowth and persistence of bacterial flora belonging normally to the nursling period. To this condition may be applied the term intestinal infantilism.

2. The chief manifestations of intestinal infantilism are arrest in the development of the body; maintenance of good mental powers and a fair development of the brain; marked abdominal distension; a slight or moderate or considerable degree of simple anaemia; the rapid onset of physical and mental fatigue; irregu-

larities of intestinal digestion resulting in frequent diarrhoeal seizures. Clinical features of secondary importance are excessive appetite, various minor signs of nervous instability, a subnormal temperature, cold hands and feet, and slight signs of rickets.

3. A study of the bacterial flora of the intestinal tract in cases of infantilism shows that the dominant bacteria of the upper and lower colon and probably of the ileum are largely Gram-positive organisms belonging to the groups of organisms which may be designated as the *Bacillus bifidus* type, the *Bacillus infantilis* type and the coccal type. It is impossible to say to what extent *B. bifidus* and *B. infantilis* constitute the dominant types, partly because of the difficulty in forming reliable estimates of the quantitative relations between these organisms, partly because they vary in the same individual under different conditions of diet and at different stages of the disease. Noteworthy is the absence of organisms of the *B. coli* and *B. lactis aerogenes* type, not only from the feces but from material collected through the use of a cathartic. The dominance of these Gram-positive organisms relates, however, only to infantilism in its incipiency and at its height.

4. Among the urinary expressions of the bacterial state associated with intestinal infantilism is to be constantly found an excess of putrefactive products of intestinal origin. Prominent among these are indican and phenol compounds. At times indolacetic acid is a prominent putrefactive product. Sometimes the aromatic oxyacids are much in excess.

5. Among the characteristic features relating to the intestinal contents are the presence of neutral fat, fatty acids and soaps in marked excess, pointing to impaired fat absorption. With this condition is associated usually an increase of mucus and other evidence of excessive desquamation of epithelial elements.

6. A careful study of the calcium and magnesium balances in one of our cases (Case I) showed failure of normal resorption of calcium and magnesium, thus accounting for the failure of skeletal growth. The amount of calcium lost by the feces as soaps of calcium was sufficient to have furnished a fair skeletal growth had these calcium soaps been absorbed instead of lost. It is a practical certainty that the loss of calcium and magnesium through the feces is the explanation of the impaired skeletal growth in intestinal infantilism.

7. In the pathology of intestinal infantilism two leading features call for explanation—first, the retardation of growth; second, the chronic intoxication. The retardation in growth can apparently be explained on the basis of the imperfect absorption of nutritive material which can be demonstrated in these cases. This impaired absorption of foodstuffs is probably to be ascribed to a chronic inflammation located in the ileum and colon and

associated with the presence of abnormal forms of bacteria. The intoxication which is so prominent a feature of intestinal infantilism at its height may confidently be ascribed to the action of putrefactive products of intestinal origin upon the central nervous system and muscles. The exact relation of the abnormal bacterial flora to the pathological conditions in the intestine is not yet clear. The chief evidence in favor of the causal relationship between the phenomena of infantilism and the overgrowth and persistence of flora of the nursling period, especially *B. bifidus*, is found in the changes that occur during convalescence when these organisms are gradually replaced by those of the type appropriate to childhood. A further evidence in the same direction is seen in the great increase in the infantile types of bacteria during periods of relapse. There is no evidence at present that intestinal infantilism has any other origin than a purely intestinal one.

8. There is a condition of acute or subacute infection of the intestinal tract in early infancy which leads to great losses in weight and strength, the persistence of which is a probable cause of chronic infantilism. This condition, like chronic infantilism, is associated with the dominance of Gram-positive microörganisms in the intestinal tract, mainly those belonging to the groups of *B. bifidus* and *B. infantilis*, or certain other acidophile bacteria which are closely related. The bacterial conditions of this acute or subacute infection, if not identical with those of chronic infantilism, are nevertheless very similar, and this is a further reason for regarding the chronic condition as the outcome of the more acute state just mentioned.

9. The state of intestinal infantilism is a very persistent one and not likely to be followed by normal growth except as the result of careful therapeutic interference. A certain proportion of such infantilism children die from acute infections of the intestine; others are permanently retarded in growth, which leads to pronounced dwarfism.

10. Rational therapeutic interference in cases of chronic intestinal infantilism offers hope of the reestablishment of the processes of growth even in cases in which the bodily arrest has been extreme and of long duration. If it is too much to say that the most satisfactory methods of treatment are now known, it may be claimed, at least, that we are in possession of certain principles of treatment which, when carefully applied, are likely to yield better results than any that have heretofore been employed.

11. Temporary relapses are very common in the course of this disease, even when great care is being taken to prevent them. The most frequent cause of such relapses is the attempt to encourage growth by the use of increased amounts of carbohydrates. When a relapse occurs the feces become voluminous, lose their

conglomerate appearance and become of lighter color. They show the presence of coccal forms in excessive numbers and there is in persistent relapses a return of *B. infantilis* and *B. bifidus.* Any disturbance of digestion which checks growth or causes loss in weight is to be accounted a relapse.

12. A permanently undersized individual is the outcome, even in the most favorably progressing instances, of the severe form of infantilism. This condition is not incompatible with a high degree of mental development.

Herter concluded that the condition resulted from the action of *B. bifidis* and *B. infantilis.* It was natural that his work should be concentrated on bacteriologic aspects of celiac disease, for that branch of medicine was then at its height, and many baffling diseases had been proved to be of bacterial origin. But none of his cases was cured, and his theories never gained acceptance. So little work was done in subsequent years along the line of Herter's ideas that there is still much that remains unknown about the possible role of bacteria in celiac disease. Kendall,[307] in 1908-09, reported on his experiments in which *B. infantilis* was fed to a dog and a monkey, resulting in diarrhea and in an increase in gram-positive intestinal organisms. But stools returned to normal in a short time.

Although Herter's conclusions failed to gain acceptance, his observations were so keen and thorough that they proved to be of great value to later workers in the field of dietary treatment. He saw that in every case proteins were very well borne, fats were borne moderately well, while carbohydrates were badly tolerated, almost invariably causing relapse or a return of diarrhea after a period of improvement. He said: "It has been already mentioned that the carbohydrates are the obvious and fruitful cause of derangements of digestion that are clinically determinable, especially diarrhoea and flatulence."

The apparent difficulty in handling fats claimed first attention then and for many years thereafter, undoubtedly because of the fatty stools which almost invariably accompanied celiac disease. Mumford,[422] in 1908, reported on several cases of "protracted non-assimilation of fat occurring in children," which seem to present typical celiac symptoms. Mumford was apparently unfamiliar with the work of Gee and Gibbons, as were so many other physicians of his day. He emphasized that there was some defect in fat metabolism which he treated with various medications including pancreatin and "non-rachitic" diet, plus massage.

In the following year Heubner [258] wrote his important paper which set the pattern for the bulk of the work done in celiac disease for many years, along the lines of dietary treatment. Heubner believed that the condition was merely one aspect of a general constitutional weakness. Noting that there was no difficulty in protein digestion, he concluded that the ingestion of fats and carbohydrates seemed to increase the severity of all symptoms. His treatment was a diet which omitted all carbohydrates and fats and was based on mother's milk. Since both offending ingredients were contained in this basic food, his patients showed little progress. However, Heubner called attention to one aspect of the disease which later workers confirmed. "One has hardly restored normal digestion through vigorous diet, than a nothing, a slight chill, the ingestion of a particle of food causes a recurrence of the diarrhea. This continues for months and for years."

In 1911 Vipond,[628] of Montreal, wrote a paper on diarrhea in children. In seeking for an improved treatment for this condition with its terrific mortality, he used banana flour (made of 70 per cent ripe banana) and plantain meal, which he described as a nourishing food, easily digested and of an astringent quality. These, with divi-divi (50 per cent tannin) reduced the frequency of the stools and tended to make them more solid in consistency. The banana flour was prepared from bananas only 70 per cent ripe and for this reason was found later to be unsuitable in the treatment of celiac disease, a condition with which Vipond was apparently unfamiliar, although there probably were some cases among those whom he treated. He stated that some of his cases had progressed for weeks at a time on banana flour, but when they returned to any other food the diarrhea recurred, ceasing again when the patients went back to banana flour. It is interesting to note in this connection that as far back as 1899, Henoch,[250] in his *Textbook of Children's Diseases*, recommended the use of another fruit—dried huckleberries—in the treatment of diarrhea. And it is well known that just before the era of the use of liver in the treatment of sprue, one of the favorite modes of therapy for this condition was the ingestion of large quantities of strawberries.

In the following decade few papers were published on the subject of celiac disease or related conditions. MacCrudden and MacCrudden and Fales,[354-359] wrote several reports in 1912 and 1913 based on chemical examinations of the urine and the feces of celiac patients. They found that creatinin was always present in the urine, was higher after ingestion of carbohydrates, lower on a high fat diet; that a large amount of calcium was lost in the feces, but that such loss was not secondary to the presence of fats or fatty acids; that the nitrogen compounds found in the feces showed that protein digestion and absorption were normal, a conclusion verified by other tests. At a time when the cause of the infantilism associated with celiac disease was under discussion, they published their belief that retardation in growth comes from a lack of material for growth rather than from a lack of the tendency to grow.

In 1918 Still [575] reported on 41 cases, 17 of which occurred among 14,800 admissions to the Great Ormond Street Hospital over a period of 5 years, and 24 of which he saw in his own practice. Herter's study of intestinal infantilism was based on 5 cases. Haas' [233] earliest series consisted of 10 cases seen during a period of 5 years: 1 in an institution, 2 in consultation and 7 in private practice. The reason for the paucity of cases reported by early workers was that only the severest cases with the classic symptoms of infantilism—

emaciation and huge abdomen—were recognized and classi-
fied as celiac disease.

Many investigators have continued to work on the analysis
of the stools of celiac patients. In 1920 Miller [389] confirmed
by careful tests the generally observed prevalence of fat in
the feces. However, in one patient whose diarrhea had
abated somewhat, the excess fat was not so great. Miller's
conviction that fat metabolism was deranged did not cause
him to exclude fats from the diet, a procedure which he
called "treating the stools and not the child." Some food
fat was absorbed, he pointed out, and gain was more rapid
when some fat was included in the diet. Although Miller's
studies indicated that there was no defect in fat splitting,
he suggested the administration of bile salts to improve this
phase of metabolism. He commented on the intermittent
character of celiac disease, concluding that its cause must
be something that waxed and waned rather than something
that came and disappeared completely. He also found that
there was no evidence of pancreatic insufficiency in his cases.
Three years later, with Perkins,[401] he reported on several
cases of what he called a "non-diarrheic" type of celiac
disease. Since the criteria for judging a celiac case were
fatty stools and inability to absorb fats properly, and since
the diagnosis was based on these symptoms alone, it is doubtful that these patients really had what we call celiac disease.

In 1920 Moorhead,[405] reporting in the *Dublin Journal of
Medical Sciences,* described two cases of infantilism, one of
which came to postmortem study. In addition to the usual
symptoms, he noticed in the first case the occurrence of
painful muscular spasms or tetany, the presence of *tricho-
cephalus dispar* in the colon, and pancreatic symptoms.
After death from an influenza attack, postmortem findings
were numerous. The uterus was extremely atrophic, and
the ovaries consisted of fibrous tissue only. The thymus was
enlarged, but the spleen, liver, kidneys, suprarenal and
pancreas were normal. The small intestine showed marked

changes; the villi showed no structure; and most of the surface portion of the mucosa had disappeared. Marked catarrh of the intestine was present; desquamated cells and mucus lay on the surface; and most of the cells of the glands showed goblet formation. The nervous system seemed to be normal except for certain changes in the pituitary gland. Moorehead concluded that the primary changes resulted from catarrh of the colon and the small intestine, and that the other changes were secondary. Moorehead treated the second case with diet and pancreatin and with other medications, since he felt that it was a case of "pancreatic infantilism" similar to that reported by Bramwell.

Meanwhile, the interest shown by Dr. L. Emmett Holt in celiac disease had been transmitted to other men beside Dr. Herter. Two young assistants of Dr. Holt at the Vanderbilt Clinic had become interested shortly after the turn of the century. They were Dr. John Howland and Dr. Sidney V. Haas, and each followed up Herter's observations independently. In 1921 Howland,[272] in his presidential address before the American Pediatric Society, read a paper on "Prolonged Intolerance to Carbohydrates." Although Howland did not use the term celiac disease (the condition was still known by a great variety of names) he described his cases as vividly as in any paper on the subject.

There are loose stools from time to time with loss of weight. The condition improves between the attacks somewhat, but sooner or later a relapse occurs and there is a renewed loss of weight. The relapses are increasingly severe. Eventually, there is a condition of marked malnutrition in a peevish, fretful, but often precocious child. The abdomen is distended, at first intermittently and then almost constantly. The stools are never normal. Even between attacks of diarrhea they are large, light gray in color, often frothy, and usually very foul. . . . All kinds of food are tried and many physicians consulted. Growth suffers in proportion to the length of time that the symptoms persist, and many children are greatly below the average in height.

Howland further stated:

From clinical experience, it has been found that of all the

elements of food, carbohydrates is the one which must be excluded rigorously; that with this greatly reduced, the other elements are almost always well digested, even though the absorption of fat may not be so satisfactory as in health.

Howland's dietary treatment consisted of three stages. The first prescribed protein milk only and lasted for a few days or weeks until the stools were formed. In the second stage, protein milk was continued, and other high-protein foods were added to the diet—curds, meat, some cheeses, and eventually eggs. "The duration of this stage," Howland wrote, "is many months, it may be years." The third stage, in which carbohydrates are added, was the most difficult period.

The addition must be made gradually with the most careful observation of his digestive capacity; it is the low carbohydrate vegetables which form a convenient starting point. . . . Bread, cereals, and potato are the last articles which can be allowed. The treatment is time-consuming, but these patients well repay the effort expended on them. They do not remain semi-invalids. Many become vigorous and strong, some even with no trace of dietary idiosyncrasies. . . . Halfway measures are quite unavailing and cause only loss of time.

Howland's treatment, which was confirmed by L. Sauer [521] in 1925, achieved greater success than any previous one, but the need for some tolerable carbohydrate in the celiac diet remained.

In November, 1923, before the section on Pediatrics of the New York Academy of Medicine, Sidney V. Haas [233] read a paper on "The Value of Banana in the Treatment of Celiac Disease," presenting 8 patients who had been cured by a high-protein diet similar to Howland's plus banana and other fruits and some vegetables which supplied carbohydrates in a form that was well borne even by advanced cases of celiac disease. Other investigators who followed confirmed the fact that the carbohydrates of banana were well tolerated by celiac patients.

In 1922 Kleinschmidt [313] devoted a portion of a general

study of diarrhea in children to the problem of celiac disease. He reported many cases showing abnormal hunger and thirst, with all interest centered upon food, and with peculiar cravings for such unusual foods as plaster, paper, coal and sand. Other children lost all interest in food or displayed temperamental eating habits, insisting on eating only from a special plate or being fed by one particular person. Kleinschmidt called these psychological abnormalities and emphasized the thesis that the children must be treated psychologically as well as dietetically. His diet was based on protein milk, with later additions of fats and carbohydrates, fruits and vegetables, the only strict omissions being those foods that fermented easily, such as honey, sugar, oatmeal and milk. Kleinschmidt reported some pathological findings: a lengthening of the bowel, a tendency toward tapeworms, and some cystic degeneration of the pancreas with shrinking of the isles of Langerhans. At a later time [314] he reported curing celiac disease by means of the diet suggested by Haas.

In 1922 Mariott [370] reported on two cases of celiac disease and expressed his opinion that the condition was purely a functional digestive insufficiency. He reported that at the height of digestion almost no hydrochloric acid was to be found in the stomach. Examination of the stools led him to believe that 90 per cent of the food fats were lost in the stools, but that even very large quantities of protein were absorbed readily. He noted that the addition of sugar to the diet led to an immediate increase in the number of stools, and he suggested that this was caused by an irritating substance that was produced during the course of the breaking down of the sugar. This substance increased peristalsis.

Marriott recommended a diet based on skimmed lactic acid milk with added milk protein plus scraped beef and certain other protein foods. He also suggested some starchy foods in the form of farina and potato, sugars in the form of corn syrup or commercial dextrin, iron, supplemental vitamins in the form of cod-liver oil, and the occasional administration of hydrochloric acid.

He pointed out, however, that this diet would not completely cure a sufferer, but that he was almost certain to suffer subsequent relapse. Even in those cases where ultimate recovery might occur, Marriot pointed out that the patient would be distinctly below normal in height, weight and general development.

Hablützel-Weber [238] published a noteworthy monograph in 1923 which reviewed the history of work on celiac disease exhaustively but made no mention of the most recent dietary suggestions made by Howland and Haas. This survey showed that there were almost as many theories concerning etiology and as many suggested treatments as there were investigators in the field. Almost the only agreement was that prognosis was bad. Hablützel-Weber also reported on 26 cases that he had studied, 4 of whom showed signs of possible neuropathology and 7 of whom showed some indications of hereditary constitutional weakness of the digestive apparatus. He noted a general secondary anemia, retarded development, especially of the long bones, and deficiency in weight. Dietary treatment consisted of the administration of a high-protein diet until diarrhea was controlled, after which there was to be gradual restoration of full diet. Taking note of the psychological aspects of the disease, Hablützel-Weber recommended a change of scene or climate whenever possible.

Ryle,[514] in 1923, noting that similar foul, greasy stools were found in celiac disease, sprue and conditions causing obstruction of the lacteals, concluded that the lacteal system might be involved in celiac disease. He suggested rigid fat restriction in the diet while such diarrhea persisted.

At about the same time Clarke and Hadfield [110] reported the case of a girl who had suffered from diarrhea for several years and showed many of the classical symptoms of celiac disease. Stools showed drops of fat but no fatty acid crystals.

A fat-free diet brought about no change or improvement. The patient died of bronchopneumonia, and postmortem findings showed atrophy of the pancreas and fatty metamorphosis of the liver. There was chronic colitis with superficial ulceration in the descending colon only.

These papers of Ryle and of Clarke and Hadfield channeled research in celiac disease into two main lines of inquiry which persisted for many years—the study of fat absorption and of the role of the pancreas. In 1925, however, Freise and Jahr [197] wrote on one aspect of the condition which had received relatively little attention. They presented clinical and roentgenologic evidence that the poor utilization of certain food elements in celiac disease was caused by a strongly increased motility of the stomach and the small intestine as well as of a portion of the proximal colon. They found that while there was very bad utilization of fat and minerals and poor utilization of carbohydrates, there was a much better utilization of proteins. They recommended the administration of opium to quiet the digestive tract and found that, as a result of this treatment, the utilization of the food elements approached normal, with subsequent improvement of the condition of the stools and striking progress in growth. Later it was found that atropine could produce the same effect. Schick and Wagner,[532] by the way, had also observed this hypermotility of the intestinal tract. Freise and Jahr were of the opinion that celiac disease was a vegetative neurosis which was only one manifestation of a constitutional weakness of the entire nervous system.

Six years later Freise and Walenta [198] reported on experiments with animals which were designed to test the earlier theories. In order to test the hypothesis that the immediate cause of the disease was a lowered tonus of the splanchnic nerve or a raised tonus of the vagus nerve, they severed the splanchnic nerve in dogs and in young swine. The experimental animals regularly developed symptoms comparable with those of celiac disease—chronic diarrhea with massive, fatty stools; increased motility of the gut; development of large abdomen; and arrested growth.

Mader,[304] in 1926, wrote along the same line, suggesting that celiac disease was a vegetative neurosis resulting in abnormal irritability of the stomach and the intestines. Since the hormones of internal secretion play an important role in the operation of the vegetative nervous system, Mader felt that the cause for the disease should be sought in the endocrine system.

In 1928 Fanconi,[172] of Zurich, wrote a paper based on 45 cases of celiac disease. His treatment substantiated the Haas thesis as to the value of fruits and vegetables, but he used buttermilk or skimmed dry milk rather than protein milk. Fanconi observed that cane sugar and grain foods, even in small quantities, had decidedly unfavorable effects, but he advised, after the first few weeks of treatment, a careful allowance of bread crust and zweiback for the dubious reason "that the child should not entirely forget how to chew."

Many physicians had noted the similarity of symptoms in celiac disease and sprue, but Thaysen,[594] in his important monograph issued in 1929, was the first to go into the subject thoroughly. He concluded that nontropical sprue and celiac disease were probably identical. He stressed the occurrence of steatorrhea in both conditions, a fact that had been emphasized by many investigators for almost two decades. Indeed, fatty diarrhea was so common and so obvious a symptom of celiac disease that until recent years it was considered an essential characteristic of the condition, if not its most salient feature.

Parsons,[447] delivering the first Rachford Memorial Lecture in 1932, drove this point home to pediatricians all over the world. His standing in the profession was so high that his conviction that fats were at fault in celiac disease won many men to the theory. Even today the opinion is widely held that fats must be excluded from the diet or reduced to a minimum, and that the origin of the ailment will finally be shown to lie in a difficulty in fat metabolism. Despite the confusion resulting from this thesis, there has been steadily increasing recognition of the primary role of disordered carbohydrate metabolism in causing celiac disease.

The work of the past two decades does not, in the main, belong in the realm of medical history but rather in the field of contemporary investigation. By the early thirties, all the existing theories concerning the etiology of celiac disease had been ably presented and could serve as a basis for further study. Furthermore, the main lines of inquiry had been laid down in the search for better treatment, more accurate diagnosis, sharper differentiation between celiac disease and other conditions presenting similar symptoms, and better understanding of the processes involved in causing the symptoms.

Two main fields for investigation existed: (1) clinical work, the chief aim of which has been to find the best dietary treatment as well as such supplements as vitamins, antibiotics, liver extract, pancreatin, etc., which might hasten recovery; (2) laboratory work, largely in chemistry and physiology, to reveal the complete picture of metabolism in celiac disease and to disclose any pathology associated with the condition. In addition to these two main types of investigation, there has also been further inquiry into the roles of the nervous and endocrine systems, the possibility of allergy as a cause, psychological aspects of the disease, and a re-examination of the role of bacteria. All the important work in these fields will be reviewed.

3

Definition

A definition of celiac disease can best be given after all evidence, both clinical and pathologic, has been presented. We shall offer such a definition in the final chapter of this work.

It may be useful, however, to present definitions which other investigators have offered. In the past all writers have defined celiac disease in terms of the most prominent symptoms or in terms of the response of the disease to specific treatment. Most of the papers on the condition, as a matter of fact, do not attempt a definition at all but rely on a description of symptoms to create a satisfactory picture of the disease, excluding, of course, other conditions with similar symptoms which can be shown to have specific causes, such as infections or infestations.

Until recent years there was relatively little disagreement. Some writers stressed one symptom more than another. Other writers did not find all of the symptoms that their predecessors had described. But in the main there was no doubt about the nature of celiac disease, even though a clear-cut definition could not be presented.

In some of the efforts that were made to subdivide the disease, confusion arose, as when Fanconi and others attempted to differentiate between celiac disease and intestinal infantilism. The same confusion exists today in the differentiation which many writers attempt to make between celiac disease and cystic fibrosis of the pancreas. As we have suggested earlier, this distinction is perhaps an academic one. So long as all pediatricians recognize that both conditions exist, it makes little or no difference if they are separate disease entities or related phases of the same basic condition.

In 1929 Thaysen [594] grouped together under the term, "idiopathic steatorrhea," tropical sprue, nontropical sprue and Gee-Herter's disease (celiac disease). He also contended that celiac disease in children was identical with nontropical sprue in adults. All of these conditions, he believed, were characterized by fatty diarrhea and were intermittent and chronic in their course and were closely related if not actually identical.

A detailed survey of the literature from the point of view of definition would serve no real purpose, since nearly all writers are equally vague and since most of them are in agreement in their vagueness. However, for frame of reference all writers on the subject may be said to be in agreement in limiting the scope of discussion to encompass a picture of chronic diarrhea, occurring in childhood and accompanied by various degrees of malnutrition.

4
Incidence

The incidence of celiac disease always has been difficult to estimate. For several decades after Gee's paper in 1888 it was considered very rare, and most reports were published on the basis of only a few cases. Heubner's [258] work was based on only 10 cases, and Hablützel-Weber's [238] on 26 cases over a period of 11 years. Still [575] pointed out that in 14,800 hospital patients under the age of 12 years, observed by him over a 5-year period, he encountered only 17 cases of celiac disease. Lehndorff and Mautner [339] emphasized the rarity of the condition, as did Stolte,[576] Czerny and Keller [124] and many others. As recently as 1934 Schiff [533] insisted that the disease was very rare and that only one or two cases a year were seen in the Berlin University Clinic.

In the last 10 or 15 years there has come a widespread feeling that the disease is actually far more common than these estimates would indicate. Increasing awareness of the condition as a specific disease has brought more frequent recognition of it. Also, more thorough understanding of varying degrees of its symptoms has revealed the existence of many mild cases, whereas only the classical severe cases had been recognized formerly. Nevertheless, it is still difficult to formulate more than a guess as to the number of sufferers from celiac disease. Pediatricians known to be interested see many more cases than others, and if calculations were based upon the number of cases they encounter in relation to their total practice a false conception of its frequency would result. On the other hand, the average physician sees so few celiac patients that many may pass him unrecognized. Since beneficial results are often not obtained quickly, frequently the patient is taken from one physician to another, thus increasing the difficulty of estimating the incidence of the disease. Although it has been stated that there is an incidence of about 2 per cent, the evidence for such a statistical conclusion is lacking.

Odegard,[435] in 1948 published the belief that celiac disease increases during and just after wartime, as figures from both the first and the second World Wars indicated. He cites reports from England and Finland to this effect and points out that in his hospital in Norway the period 1934-1939 saw only 12 patients, while a period of the same length, 1940-1945, brought 32 patients, two and a half times as many. However, the series reported is without statistical significance. The literature reveals no further information on this subject, and no explanation is offered, although dietary and emotional factors in war both suggest themselves.

Gee said that people of all ages were susceptible, but that it was especially common in children from one to five years of age, with onset starting most frequently during the second year. Almost every observer since that time has agreed with this estimate. Lehndorff and Mautner [339] said that most cases started after weaning, and others stated flatly that the disease never struck a baby being breast-fed. But our own records, and those of numerous others in recent years, show many such cases. For many years the belief persisted, however, that celiac disease never occurred under one year of age; Sidney Haas' [233] paper in 1923 made this statement. However, subsequent experience proved the error of this view. It can be stated safely now that celiac disease may exist from birth and is not at all uncommon under one year of age.

How frequently it may occur after the age of 6 is more difficult to say, Lehndorff and Mautner [339] state that there were very few cases where first symptoms occurred after the sixth year and almost none after the tenth. The literature bears this out, for almost all cases reported are those in which

symptoms started before the sixth year. It is possible, however, that with greater age the disease manifests itself in
somewhat different fashion and with less severity, so that
many cases among older persons have not been recognized.
It may be that these cases had their incipiency in childhood.
There is evidence and wide belief that in adults celiac disease is identical with nontropical sprue.

All present-day writers agree that celiac disease strikes
children of all economic groups equally. For many years,
however, the view was stated repeatedly that it afflicted the
well-to-do more than the poor. Hablützel-Weber,[238] in 1923,
commented on the number of observers who had reported
this belief; he attributed the idea to the fact that children
of poor parents received no attention and died young, so
that the cases never came to the attention of physicians.
Heubner,[258] Still,[575] and Hutchinson,[281] thought that celiac
disease was more prevalent among the wealthy because they
found it in private practice much more than in hospital
practice. But Feer,[Ad.3] Stolte,[576] Lichtenstein,[347] Kundratitz,[323]
Lehndorff and Mautner,[339] and Schiff [533] encountered most of
their cases in hospitals. Even as recently as 1938 Wall [638]
reiterated the opinion that there was greater incidence of
celiac disease among the well-to-do, which he rather curi-
ously attributed to these children being badly fed, through
having too many fats and carbohydrates loaded on their
digestive systems. Today it is agreed that the disease makes
no distinctions against the rich or the poor.

It is also generally agreed today that girls and boys suffer
from celiac disease equally, although earlier observers, such
as Still,[575] Schaap,[527] Hablützel-Weber [238] and Courtin,[118] felt
that girls were attacked more frequently than boys. Among
our own 603 cases 55 per cent were males, and 45 per cent
females.

Some evidence supports the view that there is a familial
tendency toward the disease, as Haas [233] found it in several
generations of the same family, in twins, in brothers and

sisters, in cousins and more distant relatives. But more than one case is found infrequently in the same family at the same time. Lehndorff and Mautner [339] noted that although nothing conclusive could be shown from family histories, it was astonishing, in view of the rarity of the disease, how frequently it struck close relatives—twins, siblings, cousins. Feer,[Ad 3] Hess,[255] and Sauer [521] also noted the same phenomenon. Andersen and Hodges,[17] in 1946, showed evidence that in cystic fibrosis of the pancreas there was Mendelian linkage.

Far more cases of celiac disease have been reported from England, America, Germany, Switzerland and other northern countries of Europe than from other areas, a fact which led many investigators to conclude that the disease is practically nonexistent in the Latin countries. But Schiff's [533] conjecture that the medical profession has been much more aware of the disease in those countries reporting most cases is generally accepted. With a condition as confused and in some respects so obscure as celiac disease, many cases could exist in countries whose doctors were not alert to recognize it. The great increase in the number of cases reported from South America in recent years, such as those reported in the work of Escardo [165] and Valdez y Carlos,[614] supports this view, since interest in the disease in Latin America is comparatively new.

5
Etiology

The increasingly effective studies of the past decades have brought us no closer to an understanding of the etiology of celiac disease. We might have expected at least some negative findings that would prove to be helpful by excluding from consideration some previously projected hypotheses, but every eliminated factor has found a substitute or merely moved the question one step further along on an uncharted path.

Much of the difficulty lies in the profusion of symptoms, both clinical and pathologic, reported at one time or another, and in the varying degrees of intensity of these symptoms. It has been difficult for investigators to agree upon primary and secondary symptoms; undoubtedly much of the effort to reveal the condition's etiology has been wasted upon symptoms that were secondary, although they struck the individual observer as primary.

Although the general picture and the nature of celiac disease have long been recognized without serious questioning by any worker in the field, there have been wide differences as to details. This is not surprising, for any serious digestive disturbance brings in its train a multiplicity of abnormal conditions, some of which may evidence themselves with greater apparent force than the original cause. Since many of the papers written on celiac disease have been based on only two or three cases, it is obvious that some physicians would see symptoms of which others would find no trace.

Gee, for example, thought of celiac disease as a disturbance of digestion, although he hazarded no serious guess as to the cause. Later observers assumed, from the fatty appearance of the stools, that the fault lay in fat digestion. However, chemical analysis of the stools revealed chiefly split fats, so that the problem then seemed to become one of absorption rather than digestion. In recent years there has been convincing work to indicate that fecal fat has little relation to ingested food fat. Finally, many observers now are of the opinion that steatorrhea is not an essential feature of celiac disease, no matter how common it may be.

In the search for a cause of improper digestion or absorption many workers have found an insufficiency of digestive juices only to have their findings reversed by others. Cheadle [104] very early postulated an absence or insufficiency of bile, and numerous others agreed, until further examinations proved normal biliary content. Parsons [445-451] suggested the lack of a bile salt but went on to prove its presence. Alkalinity of the digestive juices was brought forward as the reason for improper digestive function, but Neale [426-428] found that there was a normal pH. Marriott,[370] in 1922, found almost no hydrochloric acid, but many later investigators found normal amounts. Schick and Wagner [532] suggested that it was caused by a disturbance of many of the digestive glands.

And so it has gone. For almost every abnormal condition stressed by one investigator, later investigators have shown that such abnormalities were not significant. But even as late as the early 1930's, physicians were postulating a lack of bile salts and recommending their use in treatment. Only in connection with the pancreatic enzymes has there been any consistency of findings. Since Bramwell's [72] report, many physicians have regularly found a certain number of cases revealing celiac symptoms that lacked normal pancreatic enzymes or showed pathology of the pancreas on autopsy. This circumstance led very early to the belief that there were two distinct types of celiac disease, one showing pancreatic insufficiency and one that did not. A. G. Anderson and Lyall,[19] in 1933, suggested procedures by which one condition could be distinguished from the other and cited Thaysen in support. Later Farber [178-180] and also Andersen [9,10,11,13,17] did extensive work to prove that cystic fibrosis of the pancreas was a separate disease entity from celiac disease, although displaying the same clinical symptoms. Many physicians now agree with this view, but it is possible that both conditions are different aspects of the same disease. In any event the etiology of both conditions remains as obscure as ever.

Gibbons [210] was the first to suggest that the nervous system would reveal the cause of celiac disease, and numerous others have leaned to this view, including Kleinschmidt [313] and Czerny and Keller.[124] Freise and Jahr [197] felt that some weakness in the nervous system caused hypermotility of the gut, resulting in the celiac symptoms. Mader [364] agreed but carried his search one step further to the endocrine system as the controlling mechanism of the nervous system.

Other men had suggested the endocrine glands as the source of celiac disease, Eckert [151] emphasized thyroid deficiency, as did DeVille and Myers.[136] Verzar's [625] work indicated some role played by the adrenal glands, and Badenoch and Morris [28] used pituitary extract in treatment. Baggenstoss et al.[29] suggested an interesting secretion mechanism in relation to pancreatin function in cases of cystic fibrosis. But nothing at all conclusive has come from work in this field, and the general belief is that abnormal endocrine function is secondary and not a primary etiologic possibility.

Consideration of the nervous system led naturally to the suggestion of Freise and Walenta [198] that celiac disease was neurogenic. Recently, Ayers [27] and his co-workers performed splanchnicotomy on 5 cases of cystic fibrosis and preliminarily reported positive results. In this connection Farber's [179] experiments in which he produced steatorrhea in animals by administering pilocarpine are of interest. Although many physicians recognize the psychological effects of the disease and the necessity of considering these in treatment, no serious work has been done to learn if emotional factors are the ultimate cause of celiac disease.

Kundratitz,[323] who considered the nervous system a possible source of the disease, felt that any abnormality there was part of a general constitutional weakness. Heubner [258] was the first to suggest general constitutional weakness as the cause, and this view has found many supporters in a variety of interpretations. Close scrutiny of the phrase "general constitutional weakness" reveals, however, that it means nothing in the scientific sense, for it signifies only that some people get celiac disease and others do not. "Constitutional weakness" is nothing more than a way of saying, "I don't know."

This survey of etiologic theories clearly reveals the lack of unanimity among workers in the field and the absence of any progress toward an answer to the question of etiology. Since there is often wide disagreement as to the findings on which various theories are based, no general trend of thought along this line can be discerned. A survey of the literature would indicate that the only satisfactory answer at this time is that which supposes a multiplicity of causes. One expression of this view is given by Johnston and Howard [292] who point out that in a condition that may have multiple causes, thyroid deficiency is a conditioning factor in its development. It is the thought of Johnston and Howard that the "basic constitutional disease" may in some instances involve a thyroid deficiency on which is superimposed some other trigger mechanism, such as infection, allergy, or emotion. Since this thesis allows room for every etiologic hypothesis except the bacterial, most physicians will find at least some part of it to agree with. But theories that travel in so many directions at once can be of little help in our understanding or treatment of the disease.

Many inviting avenues are open for exploration in the search for the elusive cause of celiac disease. It is likely, however, that the etiology of the condition will be discovered in the course of work related to the treatment of the condition.

6

Clinical Symptoms

Almost from the beginning men agreed that not all observed symptoms of celiac disease occurred in every case, and that even the most common ones varied in degree of intensity, not only from one case to another, but also from time to time in the history of one individual case.

DIARRHEA

In describing the clinical symptoms of celiac disease, one is struck by the fact that every time a condition is cited as being commonly found, a footnote must be added stating that in some cases this condition is not only absent but that occasionally a diametrically opposite picture is presented. We meet this state of affairs even in the first symptom mentioned, the symptom which is considered the most important and characteristic—diarrhea. The stool in celiac disease has been vividly described many times as soft and mushy, far more voluminous than the intake of food would warrant, and of a particularly foul odor. The words "pasty and clayey" have been used frequently to describe the consistency of the typical celiac stool, which is generally unformed but not watery. Many physicians have added that the stool appears frothy and greasy, while all agree that usually it is decidedly pale, although different shades, ranging from pale cream to light greenish yellow, have been ascribed to it.

In the typical celiac case stools are more frequent than normal, but there is wide variation in frequency—from one to ten daily, with four or five daily being quite common.

The greasy appearance is also subject to variation. Sometimes it is so obviously fatty that droplets of oil are clearly visible to the naked eye. The stool is often mucoid, but not always.

After presenting these general descriptions with their slight variations, it is necessary to go to opposites. In rare cases there is constipation, a condition which obviously makes correct diagnosis difficult. In 1923 Miller and Perkins [401] described several cases which they called a non-diarrheic type of celiac disease. These cases presented a picture not so much of constipation as of an absence of diarrhea in the popular sense of the word. The typical pale, unformed and malodorous stool of celiac disease was not found, but rather a formed and normally colored stool. Since other symptoms of celiac disease were present, these investigators examined the stools and reported that they contained a large excess of fat, but in the form of soaps rather than the fatty acids which are found in the typical celiac stool. Since they assumed that fat absorption was the primary abnormality in the condition, they concluded that a difficulty in this stage of metabolism could exist even without diarrhea. They suggested that in quiescent or convalescent stages of celiac disease, diarrhea may cease, but poor fat absorption may be detected by analysis of the stools for fat rather than by mere inspection.

It is difficult to be certain, from their paper, whether Miller and Perkins were dealing with celiac disease or not in the cases they reported. But since later work by others has confirmed the fact that diarrhea is not an invariable concomitant of celiac disease, it is quite likely that their diagnosis was correct. In view of the reference to quiescent or convalescent stages, it is perhaps likely that the cases described by Miller and Perkins were actual celiacs who had been treated with enough success to cause subsidence of the diarrhea without improvement in the other symptoms. On the other hand, there are cases in which the diarrhea persists long after there has been marked improvement in other symptoms, such as irritability and unhappy psychological state. Most frequently, as a matter of fact, improvement in psychological state is the earliest result of proper dietary therapy. Parsons,[445] in 1930, confirmed the idea of diarrheal and nondiarrheal stages of the disease but stressed steatorrhea as the most striking symptom. In 1935 Snell et al.[561] listed steatorrhea as one of the primary symptoms but added that it might exist with or without diarrhea.

Aside from the question of steatorrhea, therefore, it may be seen that, although diarrhea is mentioned as the first and most important symptom of celiac disease, it is not an essential diagnostic criterion. Indeed, one of the characteristics of the diarrhea is that it is frequently intermittent. The attacks of diarrhea may last a few days, a few weeks, or a few months. But in most cases there are periods when it subsides, even if the patient has not been treated and is not on the path to recovery. The recurrence of diarrhea after intervals of normal or almost normal stools is so characteristic that it may be considered one of the most valuable diagnostic points available at the present time.

As for steatorrhea, Andersen,[11] in 1940 in Brenneman's system, stated that steatorrhea was a necessary diagnostic criterion for celiac disease and postulated that cases that did not show steatorrhea were not this disease but another distinct disease entity which she called starch intolerance. However, in 1947 [16] she reversed herself, stated that steatorrhea was not part of the basic disease picture and retracted the hypothesis of starch intolerance. The question of stool analysis will be dealt with more fully later.

PSYCHOLOGICAL STATE

The second most common symptom of celiac disease is a typical emotional state that is evident at once in the appearance and the behavior of the patient. The apathy, the irritability and the obvious unhappiness of the child suffering from this illness has long been noted. Kleinschmidt,[318] who was one of the first to stress the importance of psychological as well as physical treatment, described psychic abnormalities of celiac patients in regard to food and feeding. He added that these children showed no joy in play but sat dully in a corner or lay quietly.

Czerny and Keller [124] were struck by the lack of attention to the psychological aspects of celiac disease on the part of many authors. This aspect began to receive increasing attention later, and by 1934 Schiff [533] laid particular stress upon it. Like many others, he noted special symptoms in connection with food and feeding idiosyncrasies but emphasized the facial expression which, he said, seemed to lack all joy and pleasure. He also noted, among celiac patients, a concentration of interest upon themselves rather than upon things and persons around them. Refusal, he said, was the leading symptom of their nervous constellation. He pointed out that these children are frequently hypochondriacs. The complete apathy of most celiac patients, although attributed to autointoxication by Herter,[258] is considered primarily psychogenic by Schiff and by most other writers.

Such marked symptoms of irritability and apathy occur, of course, in the most severe cases. In the last decade, when more mild cases and early cases have been recognized and treated, such strong psychological symptoms have been less common. However, they may be found in some degree in almost every celiac patient. Fortunately, they are the first symptoms to disappear with proper treatment, usually clearing up within a week or two under correct diet.

APPETITE

The appetite of celiac patients is affected as much by the psychological as by the physical state. In most cases the appetite is very poor, although some patients show a good appetite.

Many authors have reported strange quirks in the appetite. Kleinschmidt [313] found that many children showed abnormal hunger and thirst, with all their interests centered upon food. He observed children who sit in the kitchen half the day and ask their mothers what they are cooking. Often these children discuss their hunger with total strangers. He also noted peculiar cravings—for wall plaster, sweepings, paper, coal and sand. On the other hand, Kleinschmidt found many children who lost all appetite and interest in food. Some would insist on eating only from a special plate or on being fed by only one person. Others insisted that their milk be strained before their eyes before they would drink it.

Lehndorff and Mautner [339] state that appetite varies greatly; sometimes there is bulemia, sometimes complete anorexia. They, too, note a stubbornness about certain foods which must be offered in strictly prescribed forms, prepared in a specific manner and served by a particular person.

Schiff [533] comments on screaming and fits of rage when food is pressed on some celiac patients, and Lichtenstein [347] observed the same thing. Stolte [576] mentioned many children who would eat only from a special plate, using one special spoon. Schiff tells of some who take only water or milk, and of others who concentrate on one particular food such as potatoes or ham. Some, he said, demand food only until it is brought into sight, whereupon they spurn it. He also mentioned children who reacted to the very sight of food with nausea and even with sitophobia.

Although extremes such as these are not frequently encountered in normal practise, the appetite is precarious. But this symptom also reacts quickly to the proper treatment, returning to normal sometimes in a matter of days. Like all the other psychogenic disturbances associated with celiac disease, the appetite peculiarities are all secondary manifestations.

GROWTH AND WEIGHT

One of the most frequent and important symptoms of celiac disease is the failure to gain weight and to grow. In severe cases there is actual loss of weight and a complete cessation of normal development. One of the most common names given to celiac disease, infantilism, indicates how frequent and striking a symptom this was in the early cases, many of which went for years without any care or with only inadequate treatment.

Gee said, "While the disease is active, children cease to grow; even when it tends to slow recovery, they are left frail and stunted." Bramwell's case was a boy of almost 19 who looked like a boy of 11 or 12. So it continued with all investigators of the condition. Clarke and Hadfield [110] reported the case of a girl over 4 years old whose weight was that of a child of 2, and whose height was that of an average 3-year-old. Many authors note that the disease is characterized by periods of improvement, alternating with periods of relapse, which are accompanied by severe loss of weight. One of our early cases weighed 17 pounds at the age of 4, and never had sat up. Most authors list defective growth as one of the essential symptoms in the diagnosis of celiac disease.

Within a few years, however, improvements in dietary therapy, including high protein intake and vitamin supplements, combined with earlier recognition of the disease, minimized the occurrence of striking growth defects. Courtin, [118] in 1933, reported on 22 children who had been treated with a fruit and vegetable diet who were given follow-up examinations from 1 to 11 years after their discharge from the hospital. In only 3 did he find any developmental retardation of the muscular and skeletal system. Many authors, however, agreed with the earlier views of Heubner, [258] Fanconi [171] and others that almost all cured cases would continue to show some retardation throughout life. Parsons, [447] too, took this point of view. Snell and others, [561] in 1935, listed loss of weight and physical stunting among the principal clinical features of celiac disease, but they indicated that patients who were seen relatively early in the course of the disease responded well to treatment and developed normally. In 1939 Hardwick [243] reported on cured cases examined after many years and stated that they tended to remain somewhat stunted.

In 1947 Andersen,[16] in listing the essential symptoms of celiac disease, noted only a "slow gain in weight" at some time. She stated her belief that osteoporosis and delay in bone maturation were among the common but not universally present symptoms. Lewes,[344] in the same year, contended that with adequate treatment and prolonged supervision there is little or no dwarfing at puberty. Our own findings, resulting from examination of celiac patients many years after cure, indicate that with treatment, utilizing proper dietary and vitamin therapy for a sufficiently long period, there is no stunting, osteoporosis, or delay in bone maturation. It is now apparent to most physicians that the early cases of poor development resulted from faulty nutrition. Diets were inadequate to maintain proper development, even when they succeeded in bringing about an apparent cure, as judged by a cessation of diarrhea.

EMACIATION AND WEAKNESS

Coupled closely with loss of weight and failure to grow are the symptoms of emaciation and weakness, and so the early observers considered the latter symptoms, too, to be almost universal. Gee spoke of a wasting of the whole body but added that "the patient wastes more in the limbs than in the face, which often remains plump until death is nigh. In the limbs, emaciation is at first more apparent to the hand than to the eye, the flesh feeling soft and flabby. Muscular weakness great: muscular tenderness often present." Cheadle described the flesh as flabby and said that in prolonged cases the patient wasted steadily to emaciation.

Lehndorff and Mautner [339] said that occasionally there was no emaciation and mentioned the full round face described by Gee. They added that when there was emaciation it was not uniform; they particularly stressed the flat buttocks commonly associated with severe cases. They also placed great emphasis on the severe weakness and tiredness of celiac patients and asserted that the cause for this lay in the nervous system as well as in the musculoskeletal system. Practically all writers on the subject stress the hypotonic musculature and the tendency to acute emaciation as among the most important clinical symptoms. As the years passed, it became increasingly clear that the wasting, the loss of muscle tone and the weakness were secondary symptoms resulting from poor nutrition. Most writers of recent years have noted that these symptoms soon disappear under proper treatment.

THE ABDOMEN

The pot belly was mentioned by all early students as an essential feature of the disease, not only in the severe cases, but also in the mild cases as well. Furthermore, they noted that the enlarged abdomen often persisted long after the disease had been brought under control. The standard texts list the protuberant abdomen as one of the essential symptoms. However, we have seen many mild cases that showed little evidence of this stigma. We have noted, as a matter of fact, that even when it is present the abdomen varies somewhat in size from day to day. However, it seems to outlast all other symptoms to the extent that patients seem to have to grow up to their abdomens before they finally become flat.

ANEMIA

Anemia has been almost universally mentioned as a symptom of celiac disease but never as a major factor. Gee and Cheadle both mentioned the pallor of their cases, and Herter, Heubner and others also found anemia to be present. Hablützel-Weber [288] reported that most of his patients presented clear evidence of hemoglobin deficiency and a picture of secondary anemia. Other authors have pointed out that while anemia was present early in the disease, examination of the blood did not reveal the degree of anemia that one might expect from the extreme pallor of the skin. Thaysen [505,601] and Svensgaard [585,586] also did much work on the blood picture in celiac disease, and both investigators found evidence of anemia. Snell and his co-workers [561] laid greater stress on the anemia than most writers have done and spoke of "anemias of various types and degrees of severity." Hassman [248] found that the blood picture was usually that of a secondary hypochromic anemia, and that isochromic or hyperchromic anemias were rarely encountered. Lewes [344] felt that anemia was present in some degree in most cases and said that it was almost invariably hypochromic in nature. Most writers agree that the anemia associated with celiac disease results from defective absorption of blood-forming elements and improves concurrently with improvement in the general nutrition.

TEMPERATURE

Gee said that sometimes the patients were hot. Hablützel-Weber [238] found that patients frequently had a low fever without any ascertainable cause. Lehndorff and Mautner [339] asserted that there was no fever associated with celiac disease except in cases where complications appeared. No present-day writers find any significant temperature connected with the ailment. When a fever exists, it no doubt arises from another condition. Since respiratory infections often precipitate celiac symptoms, any noticeable fever probably results from the infection.

PAIN AND VOMITING

Abdominal pain is not infrequent in celiac disease. Gee commented that many patients were troubled by excess wind, and all physicians since then have noted frequent cramps caused by gas and intestinal spasms. Vomiting, on the other hand, is not nearly so common, although it is not as rare as Schiff [533] and a few others have indicated. Several writers have suggested that vomiting, when it does occur, is psychogenic.

THE URINE

Herter paid considerable attention to the nature of the urine in cases of celiac disease. He found that in some cases the nitrogen content of the urine was high in proportion to the nitrogen intake of the patient. He pointed out that acetone was rarely present, but that there was excessive uric acid. Finally, he noted that the putrefaction and the decomposition that took place in the intestine showed through the urine, and that in three cases a slight reducing action with Fehling's solution was observed. Most writers who followed have found nothing significant to report in the urine of the celiac patient. Clarke and Hadfield [110] declared that it was normal. Hassman,[248] however, contended that in most cases he had found oxyacids and frequently albumin and a large amount of sediment with leukocytes, erythrocytes and granular or hyalin casts. Ødegard,[435] reporting on 27 cases, found pathologic urine in 18. He observed a small amount of protein and light pyuria when the patients were at their worst. However, the most significant work in connection with the urine has been done during the metabolic studies which will be outlined in the next chapter.

THE SKELETAL SYSTEM

Aside from the retarded development mentioned above, numerous writers have noted abnormal alterations in bone formation. Ryle,[513] in 1924, reported rickets as a common complication in celiac disease and attributed it to a calcium deficiency. However, Lehndorff and Mautner [339] made a distinction between the bone alterations caused by rickets and those caused in celiac disease, naming osteoporosis as the type of alteration found in the latter. In 1932 DeVille and

Myers [136] described a patient who could not fully extend his elbow. This condition was a result of delayed ossification. However, this difficulty was corrected when the celiac disease responded favorably to treatment.

Snell and his associates [561] said that osteoporosis occurred in connection with celiac disease and that the cause was defective metabolism of calcium and phosphorus. This contention would seem to be borne out by a recent investigation in which Vogt and Tønsager [630] found similar metabolic difficulties in cases of steatorrhea associated with adult sprue. But Hassmann,[248] in 1940, reported frequent true rachitic symptoms which he attributed to vitamin D deficiency. Parsons [443] listed osteoporosis as a common secondary condition, but noted that it occurred in the presence of normal levels of serum calcium and phosphorus and in the absence of rickets. The general feeling among pediatricians today seems to be that, despite many earlier reports of rickets and osteoporosis, neither would be encountered often with a well-balanced celiac diet containing adequate amounts of fat and proper vitamin supplements containing liberal quantities of A and D.

TETANY

Tetany has been cited by numerous writers as a complication of celiac disease. Among them are Moorhead,[416] Ryle,[513] Lehndorff and Mautner,[339] Bloch,[61,62] and Snell.[560] However, with present-day vitamin therapy tetany is encountered less and less.

MISCELLANEOUS MINOR SYMPTOMS

The list of symptoms reported at one time or another in connection with celiac disease is almost endless. A few should be mentioned, perhaps, although they are definitely of a subordinate nature and are not seen frequently now. Hydrolability, photophobia and edema are among them.

Herter,[253] Schick and Wagner,[582] and Hablützel-Weber [288] spoke of the "red tongue" of celiac disease, a condition found in many digestive disturbances. Enlarged heart, hemorrhagic states and pareses have also been listed. All are part of the picture of the classical avitaminoses and represent clinical beriberi. Practically all of the foregoing symptoms, except those referable to the gastro-enteric tract, are secondary to the celiac disease itself.

CLINICAL HISTORY

Writers on celiac disease always have searched in the family history for some etiologic clue, even for so indecisive a trait as general weakness of the nervous system or of the digestive tract. Hablützel-Weber [288] reported that of his 26 cases, 4 showed some signs of possible neuropathology in their history, and 7, signs of hereditary constitutional weakness of the digestive apparatus. Mader [363,364] reported finding some weakness of the nervous system as a hereditary feature in most of his cases. But Lehndorff and Mautner [339] felt that all statistics on the subject were inconclusive, noting that if one examined carefully enough, one could find some hereditary nervous traits in almost every child. After studying the literature carefully, they stated that there was no unanimity among authors as to whether or not the family history revealed anything significant.

Some investigators in the early part of the century found that celiac patients were born of parents in the older age group; others, that many celiac cases had siblings 10 or more years older than they. But, as a sufficient number of cases was reported, no significant variation from the normal population was found. The same result came from efforts to find a clue in the infant feeding of celiac children, although we have the impression that early feeding of solids, especially carbohydrates; may be a possible factor in precipitating the disease. Hablützel-Weber [288] reported that of his 26 cases, 75 per cent had been fed on mother's milk, while only 25 per cent were bottle-fed. Lehndorff and Mautner thought that celiac disease usually began after weaning, but concluded that this had no bearing on the condition, as the proportion of bottle-fed to breast-fed children among celiacs was the same as that in the general population. Later writers, of course, encountered many cases where the disease began before weaning, some at birth. Schiff,[533] in 1934, and other later investigators generally agreed that breast feeding had nothing to do with celiac disease, despite the fact that many early diets strongly recommended mother's milk.

There seems to be universal agreement today that if any hereditary factors exist, they are not clearly demonstrable and are of no value in diagnosis. The exception is, of course, a familial history of celiac disease itself. As noted elsewhere, evidence exists for the belief that there is some familial tendency toward celiac disease, and when there is a history of the ailment in the family, it has value in weighing the diagnosis. S. V. Haas,[235] in 1932, pointed to evidence that there is a familial tendency toward the disease. He maintained that it occurs not infrequently in several members of a family and reported cases in twins, in brothers or sisters, in cousins and even among distant relatives.

The history of the case itself is naturally of the first importance, especially in recognizing mild cases or those in which the onset is insidious. The different types of onset of the disease and the widely varying incidence and degree of the classical symptoms frequently confuse the clinical picture.

ONSET OF THE DISEASE

Even the earliest writers who observed very few cases noted the different varieties of onset. Gee wrote that "the onset is unusually gradual, so that its time is hard to fix; sometimes the complaint sets in suddenly, like an accidental diarrhea; but even when this is so the nature of the disease soon shows itself." Cheadle and almost every succeeding author noted the two types of onset, and Lehndorff and Mautner [339] described them thoroughly. They stated that in a small percentage of cases, there was some digestive disturbance from the very first day of life, but considered these cases exceptional. However, most present-day writers have noted that they are not uncommon. We have seen many such cases.

Generally, Lehndorff and Mautner pointed out, the onset is sudden or gradual. When it is sudden, celiac disease frequently starts at the end of another disease—grippe, pneumonia, pertussis, or even after vaccination or dentition. Later writers stressed respiratory infections as leading to the onset of celiac disease and dismissed earlier investigators' ideas about the role of dentition. A large number of cases show diarrhea as a first symptom following an upper respiratory infection, often a mild one.

As for the many cases—perhaps the majority—of gradual and insidious onset, Lehndorff and Mautner pointed out that the first symptoms were usually digestive, but not always so. In some cases behavioral symptoms came first; sometimes vomiting was the earliest symptom, although it is uncommon in the full-fledged disease. Some cases, they noted, began with constipation. In most cases, however, gradual onset started with the classic symptoms in mild degree—diarrhea, voluminous and foul stools, loss of appetite, retardation of growth and weight-gain. In some cases, these symptoms were so mild at the beginning that parents paid little attention to them until a sudden accidental complication, such as bone fracture, tetany, etc., brought the true situation to light.

Most writers have called attention to this variation in manner of onset. In some cases of insidious onset the voluminous stool may appear before diarrhea, loss of appetite and loss of weight. Lewes,[344] in emphasizing the insidious onset in so many cases, said that the slightness of first symptoms often delayed the beginning of treatment after diagnosis. Our own experience has confirmed the importance of the history of the case and the necessity of considering celiac disease as a possibility, even in the absence of the classical symptoms or in cases showing only some but not all of the most common symptoms. Certainly a history of anorexia, intermittent, recurrent diarrhea, with intervals of weeks or months during which the child does fairly well despite an overall failure to gain weight or to grow normally—such a history must suggest celiac disease, among other possible considerations, as a most likely diagnosis.

7

Pathology

GENERAL POSTMORTEM FINDINGS

In no other aspect does celiac disease give evidence of its variability and contradictions so strongly as in the reported postmortem findings. Here is a disease, apparently of the digestive apparatus, with many strong and violent symptoms, resulting in extreme emaciation and often death without proper treatment. It would seem almost inconceivable that such a disease would fail to reveal obvious and major alterations in the digestive apparatus. Yet this has been the case. When pathologic conditions have been found, they have not been found in all cases, and generally they have appeared to be secondary.

Gee said that "nothing unnatural can be seen in the stomach, intestine, or other digestive organs." Other early writers agreed, in the main, except for several instances of pathology of the pancreas. Here we examine the general findings of writers who have reported postmortem examinations in sufficient detail to indicate the variety and the inconclusiveness of these findings.

Moorhead,[416] in 1920, reported many pathologic conditions: uterus atrophic, ovaries consisting only of fibrous tissue; thymus enlarged and consisting mainly of fat; thyroid slightly enlarged but otherwise normal; spleen, liver and suprarenals normal. Despite much early belief that liver function must be disturbed in celiac disease, Moorhead found the liver normal, and also the pancreas, which has shown pathology to so many investigators. However, he found that the small intestine showed marked changes. The villi showed no structure, and most of the surface of the mucosa had disappeared. There was marked catarrh of the intestine; desquamated cells and mucus lay on the surface; and most of the cells of the glands showed goblet formation. The nervous system appeared to be normal, except for the pituitary, the anterior portion of which revealed a looser and more irregular structure, especially at the periphery. In some sections the eosinophil cells were replaced by large gray cells, lining the walls of the spaces or collected as groups inside. Also, there were many more of the small cells with small quantities of unstained protoplasm around the nucleus. There was little colloid in this part of the gland; what there was, stained yellow. Moorhead stated that the apparently primary pathologic change in his case was catarrh of the colon and probably of the small intestine. The other changes, he indicated, were probably secondary.

In 1922 Kleinschmidt [313] reported a lengthening of the bowel, cystic degeneration of the pancreas and shrinking of the isles of Langerhans. In 1924 Clarke and Hadfield [110] found atrophy of the pancreas in a girl aged 4 years and 4 months who began to have fatty diarrhea at 5 months (a typical celiac) and died of bronchopneumonia following nasal diphtheria. The pancreas consisted of fat and only about one twentieth of normal gland tissue, which was still active but appeared to be undergoing slow replacement fibrosis. It contained islet tissue in more than normal amount, but there was no clear evidence of pancreatitis. They also found fatty metamorphosis of the liver, unaccompanied by any sign of hepatic necrosis, clear-cut cholangitis, or pylephlebitis. There was also chronic colitis, with superficial ulceration in the descending colon only.

Marriott [370] reported in 1922 that there were no consistent pathologic findings; that, although the liver may be small, the pancreas occasionally slightly atrophied, and the intestines distended, even these conditions were far from universal.

Lehndorff and Mautner [339] reviewed the findings of other authors and expressed surprise that such a long-lasting and severe illness as celiac disease should reveal so few pathologic changes. They commented upon some observations of a general thickening of the gastro-intestinal tract, a congestion of the mucosa, prominent follicles in the large intestine, in addition to microscopic observation of an infiltration of the mucosa and the submucosa of the stomach and the small intestine with small round cells. Occasionally there was increase in connective tissue and extravasated blood. They noted occasional fatty degeneration of the liver, but pointed out as the most important changes those that occurred in the pancreas. Here they found degeneration of the parenchyma, reduction of the cytoplasm of the cells lining the ducts, and a definite increase in the interlobular connective tissue, especially in the tissue that surrounds the excretory ducts. But there was no indication that this condition was primary.

In 1928 Bloch [61] stated that anatomic investigations showed that tissues were everywhere intact. There was no ulceration, destruction or degeneration. Microscopic search showed the existence of subchronic inflammation in the stomach and the intestines, with a large amount of mucous cells in the walls of the colon. The glands were preserved in stomach, intestines, pancreas and liver. The parietal cells in the gastric glands were without primary capillaries, and in only a few secretory cells were any granules to be found.

Macrae and Morris [362] in 1931 could find no evidence of any structural change in the intestines to account for the grave defect in absorption, which they considered at the heart of celiac disease. Two of their cases showed nothing at all, and one showed some atrophy of the liver and the spleen. But they agreed with Lehndorff and Mautner that all these observed changes were due to the hunger condition of the patient.

In 1946 Allibone [5] reported an enteritis and otitis media, with a terminal bronchopneumonia. There was atrophy of the secretory tissue of the pancreas and increase of connective tissue. Tiny patches of demyelinization of the posterior columns of the spinal cord were seen, with hydropic degeneration of the heart muscle, which suggested beriberi. Despite the emphasis that many writers placed on the pancreas, Allibone could not be certain whether the changes there were primary or secondary. With the possible exception of the pancreas, all postmortem findings are considered today to be secondary. In the case of the pancreas, as we shall see, several important investigators believe that these alterations indicate not celiac disease but rather a distinctly different condition showing similar symptoms. They named this condition cystic fibrosis of the pancreas.

Still,[575] in 1918, reported thickening of the bowels in areas of congestion as well as prominent solitary follicles. He found that the liver was large, pale, soft and fatty. Microscopic examination revealed round-cell infiltration of the mucosa and the submucosa more frequently in the stomach and the small intestine rather than in the large intestine. The pancreas showed a marked increase in interlobular fibrous tissue, particularly in the areas surrounding the ducts.

In 1928 Fanconi[171] reported on 6 cases that were studied at autopsy. The findings in the gastro-intestinal tract indicated intensive resorption of fat in the intestines. The liver findings were normal, as were those for the pancreas, and in only one case was there severe atrophy of the thyroid gland. There were no suggestive changes in the vegetative nervous system. Osteoporosis and the cross striation of the metaphysis as a result of periodic changes in the intensity of bone formation were the most characteristic bone findings. He could find no morphologic basis for the digestive insufficiency. The pathologic anatomic findings, furthermore, indicated that the abnormalities were secondary and the result of the intermediary metabolism and of the anemia. These findings gave the picture of a child who had gone hungry for a long time. In a later study,[177] he reported a combination of the celiac syndrome and the typical pulmonary involvement with fibrosis of the pancreas. Knauer,[316] too, in 1935, maintained that the pathologic-anatomic findings in celiac disease are, as a rule, secondary. With this conclusion, most investigators who have studied this aspect of the disease are in almost complete agreement.

In 1935 Hess and Saphir [256] reported strikingly similar findings in 3 cases that came to postmortem. All revealed bronchopneumonia of recent development, chronic enteritis and severe changes in the pancreas. Histology of the lungs showed the alveoli with large monocytic cells which were filled with fat. There was no atrophy of thymus, thyroid or suprarenals. Chronic lesions were found, principally in the small intestines. Grossly, the pancreas showed no noteworthy changes, but histologically the changes were marked, indicating a severe fibrosis with dilated ducts and scattered lymphocytic infiltration in two cases. In all three cases evidence of regeneration of the pancreas was demonstrated by the presence of mitotic figures and by the appearance of syncytial cell masses.

In the same year Parmelee,[442] reporting on two cases that came to autopsy, found marked fibrosis and a great diminution in the amount of secretory gland tissue in the pancreas, bronchopneumonia, and sometimes numerous widely disseminated miliary abscesses and changes in the alveolar walls indicative of chronic irritation. Poynton and his co-workers [466] noticed an increase in the interlobular fibers of the pancreas. Passini [450] found cystic degeneration of the pancreas, with some atrophy and necrosis. Schick and Wagner [582] reported atrophy of many glands and of the mucosa of the duodenum. Pipping [458] noted fatty changes in the liver. Potter [Ad.11] discovered a slight thickening of the mucous membranes of the intestines and occasionally small-cell infiltration and fibrosis around the pancreatic ducts. Gross [230] found almost complete atrophy of the parenchyma of the pancreas, combined with fat infiltration, as well as an increased number of islets. Levinsohn [342] reported atrophy and fatty degeneration of various endocrine and digestive glands which, he pointed out, were changes usually found in starvation and avitaminosis. However, it is important to note that none of these investigators ever adduced evidence that there was a direct and causal relationship between these structural changes and celiac disease.

BACTERIOLOGY

Herter found that the bacteria in the stools of sufferers from celiac disease were predominantly gram-positive "aciduric" organisms with an absence of the colon group, and that they retained their infantile characteristics. He pointed to the existence of B. *bifidis* and B. *infantilis* and further observed that the number of these organisms varied directly with the acuteness of the symptoms. In general, Herter's findings have not been accepted as an explanation of the etiology of the disease, although Brown and his collaborators [86] found that a predominantly gram-positive "aciduric" intestinal flora of B. *bifidis* type was characteristic of chronic intestinal indigestion, and that such a typical intestinal flora, unusual for the stage of life in which celiac disease occurs, is strongly suggestive of a bacterial influence in the etiology of the condition.

In 1909 Kendall [307] reported on his finding of a spore-forming organism, B. *infantilis*, in each of a series of cases of infantilism. He noted, however, that they were also found in limited numbers in the feces of some normal infants. "B. *infantilis*," he said, "is not an obligate intestinal bacillus, but a saprophytic organism which, under certain undetermined conditions, finds suitable environment in the intestinal tract where it proliferates." Kendall observed that it produced no agglutinins, and that there was no direct evidence to indicate an etiologic relationship to infantilism or celiac disease. However, when it was fed to a dog and a monkey, *B. infantilis* caused a pronounced softening of the stools and a diarrhea. In the monkey the latter was followed by a decided diminution in the gram-negative, gas-producing bacilli of the coli-aerogenes type, and a marked increase in the gram-positive acidophilic flora. *B. bifidis* in moderate numbers and *B. acidophilus* in excessive numbers were the dominant organisms. There was a gradual return to normal stools, as shown by both macroscopic and microscopic examination. Kendall felt that his experiments furnished evidence that diarrhea in celiac disease may be caused by irritant metabolic products, resulting from the proliferation of *B. infantilis* in the intestinal tract. In a later paper he discusses the adaptation in the intestine to long-continued carbohydrate feeding on the part of spore-bearing bacilli.

Few writers went further with bacteriologic studies. However, Blühdorn [64] felt that celiac disease was "an endogenous infection of the small intestine." Schiff and Kochmann [534] spoke of a revival of the bacterial theory of etiology of acute nutritive disease, citing Moro's contention that in such diseases the normally bacteria-poor small intestine showed a wealth of bacterial flora. Bessau [51] substantiated Moro's thesis.

Schiff and Kochmann pointed out that many workers had looked for the cause of acute diarrhea in infants in abnormal acid formation in the intestine, Bokai having postulated that certain fatty acids irritated the gut, Bahrdt and Bamberg maintaining that acetic acid caused abnormally strong peristalsis. In searching for the cause of abnormal acid formation, Schiff and Kochmann considered the bacterial fermentation of sugars, as well as the bacterial destruction of fat, a process about which little was known. They cited Bessau's work as showing that it was not abnormal fermentation that caused nutritive disorders, but rather the fact that such fermentation took place in an abnormal place. This contention gains significance when we recall that large numbers of acid-building *B. coli* are found in endogenous infection of the small intestine.

Schiff and Kochmann performed some interesting experiments on the operation of *B. coli* in the small intestine, indicating that proteins were attacked by *B. coli* to produce amines, the reaction occurring in a sugar-free nutrient medium or at the same time that sugar fermentation occurred. The presence of fats or the salts of the higher fatty acids, they claimed, favored bacterial growth. Schiff and Kochmann postulated that the small intestine was sterile under normal conditions, but that if something occurred to block the chyme, there would then be a suitable medium for bacterial growth. Any fermentable carbohydrates in the small intestine would then begin to ferment, and even proteins, especially the products of their destruction, would be attacked by the intestinal flora.

Recalling that under normal conditions amines are built in the intestinal tract through bacterial action, Schiff and Kochmann suggested that in acute nutritive disorders the organism could not take care of the toxic nature of the amines. Such toxicity, therefore, could only be secondary to a primary cause of the disorder. They assumed that the primary cause lay in the intermediate metabolism and was probably a hindrance of oxidation.

Schiff and Kochmann suggested that children whose digestive disorder was primarily a fat intolerance showed these symptoms because fats and the salts of the higher fatty acids promoted bacterial growth. Since the existence, or at least the degree, of fat-intolerance in celiac disease is now seriously questioned, this suggestion may have little value. But other questions brought up by the work of these investigators, notably the bacterial production of a material having a toxic effect on the intestine, may well merit further investigation. However, most of the work on metabolism since Schiff and Kochmann reported has taken a different turn, and comments on the role of bacteria have been chiefly in the nature of remarks noted in passing.

Wall,[638] following Kahn,[296] pointed out in 1938 that banana powder, which he found so useful in the treatment of celiac disease, seemed to change intestinal bacterial flora to a gram-positive type, lending support to Herter's theories. Von Meysenburg and Fine [635] had noted the same fact two years earlier.

In 1940 Hassmann [248] presented some interesting suggestions in connection with the bacterial factor in celiac disease. His observations are confused by the fact that he, like Fanconi, made a distinction between celiac disease and intestinal infantilism. He maintained that in children who had only chronic constipation without any diarrhea, only bacteria of the coli group could be found, and there was no evidence of endogenous infection, the symbiotic balance between the intestinal flora being maintained. In celiac disease he found atypical Paracoli bacteria both before and after attacks of diarrhea. These bacteria disappeared, or at least diminished, in periods between attacks, only to return when another diarrheic attack occurred. In what he called intestinal infantilism, Hassmann maintained that the atypical bacteria persisted as long as the disease continued, whether or not there were attacks of diarrhea. Infantilism was thought to be, therefore, a disorder of symbiosis, curable—strikingly enough —by a banana-and-apple diet. This diet, Hassmann believed, cleaned the intestines out by mechanical means and reestablished symbiotic balance.

Although other writers now make other distinctions and divide celiac disease into two or more diseases, this particular distinction of Hassmann's, between celiac disease and intestinal infantilism, apparently has found no followers in the literature. Most writers today would consider his two diseases as one, celiac disease displaying differing symptoms and thus different pathologic findings only in the matter of degree.

Many other writers have treated the relationship between bacteria and celiac disease, but only casually and at times tangentially. Farber,[178] in writing on pancreatic insufficiency which displayed the celiac syndrome, suggested the possibility of a filterable virus as the cause, but then he proceeded to prove that evidence of such infection occurred no more frequently in his pancreatic cases than in the general population. Torrey [610] showed that in dogs, increase in acidophilus flora follows feeding of lactose and dextrins. Fiori [184] reported that in rabbits the introduction of staphylococcus toxin exerts a hypoglycemic effect, and that intravenous injections of dextrose immediately after inoculation prolong the life of the animal and attenuate symptoms of poisoning. Kahn [296] found that the introduction of banana powder to the diet of infants resulted in the conversion of the intestinal flora from an almost completely gram-negative state to an almost equally completely gram-positive state. Elvehjem and Krahl [158] contended that the extent to which a favorable bacterial synthetic mechanism can assist man in supplying certain factors may depend on the type of carbohydrate employed in the diet. Schütz,[537] who is credited with being the first writer to call attention to celiac disease in Germany, believed that the normal intestine regulated the growth of bacteria in many ways, while the diseased intestine somehow lost this ability. Rettger and Cheplin [480] adduced evidence to show that diet is a controlling factor in the regulation of the bacterial activity in the intestinal canal of albino rats and showed parallel results in human subjects. Porter et al.[464] attributed pancreatic insufficiency to a bacterial invasion secondary to the presence of an abnormal bacterial flora in the intestines. Tepley and his co-workers [592] showed that antibiotics inhibit the growth of intestinal bacteria and showed, also, that while there was a large amount of niacin and folic acid per gram of cecal contents in rats on a dextrin diet, there was little synthesis of either vitamin on lactose. Weinstein and Weiss [643] studied the influence of certain dried fruits and absorbing agents on the intestinal flora of white mice.

While none of these investigations has produced conclusive evidence of an etiologic connection between bacteria and celiac disease, they have opened up extremely valuable paths for further investigation.

8

Roentgenographic Evidence

Most writers have agreed that x-rays of celiac patients show a typical moulage pattern, but this is found in some normal children and in other deficiency states and is therefore of little use.

In 1948 Møller and his associates [409] presented what is probably the most complete and up-to-date report in this field. They examined 275 children, 63 of whom were celiac cases, 25 were normal, and 167 were suffering from other digestive disturbances. Each child was examined several times, some as many as eight times. The total number of roentgenograms exceeded 2,100. In celiac disease there was evidence of an abnormal motor function of the small intestine. The most prominent feature was an abnormal tonus of the bowel, segments with hypotonia alternating with hypertonic segments. These abnormal conditions were of long duration, often persisting for several months after clinical improvement. These roentgenologic findings were not obtained in the other gastro-intestinal disturbances.

Golden [219] points out that abnormal intestinal patterns are found in celiac disease as well as in other digestive disorders. He states that during the first months of life the normal intestinal pattern is identical with the abnormal patterns of well-advanced deficiency states and adduces evidence that the primary causal mechanism of the abnormality is in the intramural nerve plexuses. He points out that while a differential diagnosis cannot be made from the roentgen findings alone, an evaluation of the roentgen changes in the light of other clinical information may clarify the significance of the functional abnormalities of the small intestine.

Gonce [220] as well as Kantor [298] have shown that there are rather definite roentgenographic changes associated with celiac disease, but no author has been able to report any clear roentgenologic evidence that would be of real diagnostic or therapeutic value or that would give a really significant hint as to etiology.

9

Digestion and Absorption

PROTEINS

Some of the earliest writers on celiac disease suggested that there might be abnormalities in protein digestion associated with the illness. Heubner,[258] for example, recommended low-fat and low-carbohydrate diet in most cases, and in severe cases also eliminated proteins. Specifically, there were three ideas about protein metabolism—that the proteins were split too rapidly, that they formed unabsorbable derivatives, or that they were absorbed imperfectly. But clinical experience has proved that there is no difficulty in protein metabolism or utilization. MacCrudden and Fales,[355,356] in two of their series of papers on metabolism in celiac disease, showed conclusively, through a study of nitrogen content of the feces, that proteins were well digested and well absorbed. All subsequent experience has confirmed this and has even emphasized the desirability of larger than normal protein intake in the celiac diet.

The question of protein metabolism in celiac disease, although not yet completely answered, has been thoroughly pursued. West, Wilson, and Eyles [648] have shown that there is some impairment of the utilization of blood amino nitrogen in infants with impaired pancreatic function. Shohl and his colleagues [553] have demonstrated the value of enzymatic hydrolysate of casein in impaired pancreatic function. A. G. Anderson and Lyall,[19] in their work, indicate that the character of the food nitrogen has some influence on the digestion and the absorption of that element.

Badenock and Morris [28] stated that the absorption of a simple nitrogenous compound is not impaired in celiac disease and that the excretion of urea is normal. Rather than supporting the old hypothesis that there was an abnormality of protein metabolism in celiac disease, all recent research has pointed toward the use of protein-rich diet in the treatment of the ailment.

FATS

The very obvious evidence of oily or greasy stools in celiac disease naturally led all early writers to assume that the chief trouble in the illness lay with the digestion or absorption of fats. Chemical examination of the feces strengthened this view. In 1920 Miller [889] reported on his work on three cases: two in a state of active diarrhea, one in a quiescent state with formed stools. The first two showed percentages of fat in dried feces of 57.14 and 52.4. The third showed fecal fat slightly above normal—24 to 28 per cent. Miller further noted that increasing the daily fat intake when the case was quiescent increased not only the absolute amount of fat absorbed but the percentage of food fat. As a result he added some fat to his diet, even though this made the stools slightly soft, because of the greater fat absorption. Only in severe cases did he eliminate this nutrient.

Miller learned, too, that there was no defect in fat splitting, indicating that the fault must lie in absorption rather than digestion. Administration of bile salts seemed to increase the splitting of fats somewhat in active cases, so he recommended its use.

Three years later Miller and Perkins [401] wrote their paper on the "nondiarrheic" type of celiac disease, stating that they found formed and colored stools with more than 50 per cent fat in the form of soaps. When fat appeared in the feces as fatty acids, the stools were the typical celiac kind.

Marriott [870] reported similar conclusions, showing that fecal fat in the inactive stage of the disease consisted chiefly of soaps. He also stated that in celiac disease the absorption of fat from food was less than 10 per cent. Lehndorff and Mautner [339] concluded from their studies of metabolism in celiac disease that fat as well as carbohydrates, water, albumen and all salts were absorbed defectively. Kundratitz,[020] in 1927, confirmed the fact that stools contained split fats, indicating that any fault was in absorption rather than digestion, and Telfer,[591] the next year, made a similar report.

But some writers doubted that faulty fat absorption told the whole story or even a large part of it. Howland [272] and Haas,[235] among others in the clinical field, were stressing carbohydrate intolerance as more significant. In the laboratory Muncrieff and Payne [423] studied blood fat in celiac disease and found higher fat content than in normal individuals. This suggested that the difficulty was in the intermediate metabolism, and that possibly the high blood fat hindered absorption or promoted re-excretion into the intestine. On the other hand, Fanconi [170] reported a low blood-fat curve which was even flatter after oral administration of olive oil.

Parsons [445] also found the blood fat generally lower in celiac disease and could discern no evidence to support the view that increased fecal fat represented increased excretion of blood fat, disputing Bauer [39] on this point. He cited his cases which showed fecal fat of 22.5 to 74.5 per cent, most of them with 40 to 50 per cent of fat in dried feces. In spite of this, Parsons pointed out, the percentage absorption of fat was surprisingly high. In the nondiarrheic phase of the disease he found that increase of fat intake brought increase of fat absorption, but he warned that continued intake of much fat would bring return of diarrhea.

Macrae and Morris [362] investigated the question of blood fat in 1931 and found it difficult to obtain blood in different individuals when the intermediate metabolism of fat was at the same stage, since the various conditions affecting the migration of fat to and from the tissues was largely unknown.

However, their estimates of blood fat in several cases indicated that all the values were within the normal range, but normal range is admittedly very wide. Macrae and Morris considered the thesis of Freise and Jahr [197] that defective fat metabolism was due to rapid passage of chyme through the intestine. They followed, in two cases, the passage of a barium meal radiographically but noted no abnormality in the times taken to complete the various stages. In addition, carmine or charcoal ingested orally appeared in the feces no more rapidly than in normal infants. They concluded that the abnormality in celiac disease was not in the intermediate metabolism, in the intestinal contents passed, but rather seemed to lie in some physicochemical abnormality of the intestinal contents. Macrae and Morris investigated this thesis, rejecting the previously presented notion that lack of bile caused poor fat utilization, but feeling that there was some evidence supporting the efficacy of bile salts, although it was far from conclusive. They found, however, that acid sodium phosphate promoted fat and mineral metabolism, probably because of its acid nature. They concluded that perhaps the celiac intestine had a pH of less than 9.0, causing defective absorption of minerals and defective flow of bile. Shift of the reaction to the acid side would thus facilitate the absorption of lime and phosphorus and also increase the amount of bile which would raise the utilization of fat. With increased fat absorption, more vitamin D would be absorbed, causing the fixation of the calcium and the phosphorus in the bone. All this work was based on the thesis that was already being seriously questioned by numerous writers. Schlesinger and Keele,[535] in 1935, reported on a case of celiac disease that, in addition to the usual symptoms, presented rickets and symmetric fractures. They found that fat metabolism was normal but that the striking feature was a disordered carbohydrate metabolism.

Many writers continued to concentrate on fats as the villains in celiac disease. Snell et al.,[561] in 1935, stated that the difficulty lay in the absorption of fat. Numerous investigators, although holding to the thesis of defective fat metabolism, agreed that carbohydrate metabolism was also defective. Gonce,[220] in 1942, reported finding dried feces with from 50 to 70 per cent of fat and concluded that around 50 per cent of fat intake was lost in the stools. But he added that all fat need not be excluded from the diet.

At this time many writers were making a distinction between two conditions showing the celiac set of symptoms—celiac disease and cystic fibrosis of the pancreas. Farber[178-180] wrote many reports indicating that duodenal contents revealed which of the two conditions existed. Andersen[16] followed the same thesis and in a report published in 1947 stated that steatorrhea was not an essential feature of celiac disease. She felt that in celiac disease fat absorption could no longer be called the chief abnormality. She pointed out that though the transitory steatorrhea is a complication due to specific deficiency of vitamins, the main therapeutic requirement of celiac disease was a diet high in protein, low in starch and abundant in vitamins. As to fats, she specifically stated that moderate amounts may be supplied to patients in good condition. This is in contrast with her article in Brennemann's System,[11] in 1940, in which she ascribes the clinical picture of celiac disease as due to fat intolerance and therefore rigorously excludes all fat from the diet. In 1946 Scott[545] made the statement that fecal fat bore no relationship to the fat ingested in the food. Other observers had found that there was fecal fat on a completely fat-free diet.

Because of the obvious evidence of fat in the feces in celiac disease, there has been an enormous amount of research into the problem of fat metabolism over the course of the years. While it is impossible to summarize all of the work that has been done, a cross section of the research will be of value in indicating general trends. Holt, Sr.,[265] one of the earliest investigators, found no definite relationship between

daily fat intake and the per cent or distribution of fat in the
stool. Mendel [381] observed that in normal experimental rats
the addition of butter or butter fat to the diet prevented the
suspension of growth in immature animals and promptly
restored growth when it had failed. Lewis and Lough [345]
reported that fat absorption may be greatly impaired in
severe diarrhea, but Hill and Bloor [261] accounted for the
excess fecal fat by considering it to be a product of intestinal
secretion or excretion rather than a failure of absorption.
In respect to the intermediate metabolism of fat, the older
theory of Van Slyke stated that the human organism
appears to be incapable of oxidizing the common fatty acids .
unless a certain amount of carbohydrate or other material
capable of forming glucose is burned simultaneously, and
Shaffer has adduced evidence that the influence of carbohydrate in facilitating the combustion of fat follows a quantitative law. Whether or not the older theory in regard to
the burning of fat in the fire of the carbohydrates can be
given credence, the fact remains that in celiac disease, a diet
high in carbohydrates acceptable in this disease makes it
possible to ingest fats in practically any normal quantity
without apparent disturbance—a condition which did not
exist before special carbohydrates were given. Brown [85]
pointed out that fats vary in their ability to be utilized by
the organism, showing evidence, for example, that cod-liver
oil contains certain long-chain, highly unsaturated fatty acids
that are not readily burned and that tend, therefore, to
accumulate in the liver. Bauer,[39] too, reported that animal
fat is probably more readily digested than vegetable fat, and
that children who suffer from celiac disease have no more
difficulty in absorbing fats than do normal children. Shapiro
and his co-workers contended that the fecal lipids may
consist largely of fatty material secreted into the bowel rather
than unabsorbed food lipids. Adlersberg [2] found that the
addition of lecithin enhances the elevation of the total lipids
of the serum in the fat tolerance test, and of the vitamin A

content of the serum in the vitamin A tolerance test; therefore, he recommended the use of moderate amounts of lecithin in the diet of celiac disease and other manifestations of
the so-called "sprue syndrome." Wollarger and his associates [652] pointed out that, although increase of dietary fat and
protein causes an increased wastage of these nutrients in the
feces, it also resulted in an increased assimilation of the food
elements. Holt, Jr., and his colleagues [268] believed that there
appeared to be a definite relationship between absorption
and unsaturation, the unsaturated fats being absorbed more
readily. Rony and Ching [503] performed experiments from
which they concluded that carbohydrate metabolism plays an
important if not an essential role in the regulation of the
blood-fat level of normal dogs during the alimentary absorption of fat. Burr observed that normal growth and health
of rats requires the presence of certain unsaturated fatty acids
in the diet. Best and Taylor [52] reported that even in the
absence of the pancreas or in the ligation of its ducts, relatively large amounts of fats may be digested. Various investigators have shown that the normal gastro-intestinal mucosa
is able to excrete fat itself even on a completely fat-free diet
and during starvation. Chung,[107] as well as Holt, Jr.,[268]
observed that a high fat intake brings about a greater absolute amount of fat absorbed even in nutritionally abnormal
patients; he points to the significance of this fact in view of
the prevalent use of low-fat formulas in the treatment of
diarrhea, a regimen "which may contribute to nutritional
failure."

Despite the increasing evidence in the laboratory as well
as the clinic that fat tolerance is not the chief problem in
celiac disease, many writers and pediatricians continue to
feel that fat must be rigidly restricted in the diet.

CARBOHYDRATES

Early clinical observations that carbohydrates were poorly
tolerated in celiac disease received little notice from most

writers, and little work on carbohydrate metabolism was done in comparison with the amount of study on fat digestion and absorption. Marriott,[370] in 1922, in reporting on the amount of fat in the feces, noted incidentally that when sugar was added to the diet, there was an almost immediate increase in the number of stools. This led him to conclude that fermentable sugars produced a substance which irritated and increased peristalsis, but no metabolic studies were made to verify this idea. Lehndorff and Mautner [339] made the most thorough studies done up to that time and concluded that water, fat, carbohydrate, albumen and all salts were poorly absorbed through the intestinal tract. Kundratitz,[328] in 1927, examined the duodenal juices in two cases and found normal concentrations of enzymes for fat, carbohydrate and protein digestion, lending support to the widely accepted view that whatever food element was at fault in celiac disease, the difficulty lay in absorption rather than in digestion.

Despite a mounting array of evidence from clinicians that carbohydrate intolerance was the primary difficulty in celiac disease, metabolic studies continued to be almost exclusively in the realm of fats and minerals. Macrae and Morris,[362] in 1931, published an excellent paper on metabolism in celiac disease and noted that carbohydrates were absorbed with more difficulty than normal, but they went no further. After attention had been called to it by Thaysen [595] and Svensgaard,[585,586] numerous writers noted that in celiac disease the blood sugar curve was flat. But this, of course, held true in many different disturbances of the digestive tract and in other conditions as well. Schlesinger and Keele,[585] in 1935, reported that while they found fat metabolism to be normal, there was striking disorder of carbohydrate metabolism. They found that the blood-sugar curve, after a few days' regular administration of glucose and insulin, approached normal. The treatment was continued, with interruptions, for 7 weeks, during which the general condition of the patient showed remarkable improvement. When insulin and glucose treatments were stopped and a regular diet reinstituted, progress continued, but the blood-sugar curve reverted to the flat type. Oral administration of the normal test amount of glucose, 25 Gm., showed no change in the curve, nor did dosages of 50 or 100 Gm. Only when a dose of 250 Gm. was administered did the blood-sugar curve show an appreciable rise.

Schlesinger and Keele then undertook experiments to learn if the flat blood-sugar curve might be due to faulty carbohydrate assimilation. The patient was given an ordinary diet plus 100 Gm. of glucose for 3 days. After a suitable period, the experiment was repeated, using 250 Gm. of glucose. Passage through the intestines was followed in each case by a charcoal marker, and the feces were collected and analyzed for soluble carbohydrates. At the same time, blood-sugar estimations were made regularly. Urine tests throughout the experiment failed to show any glycosuria, and fecal carbohydrate was negligible—over 97 per cent being absorbed. Schlesinger and Keele concluded, therefore, that lack of absorption from the digestive tract could not be responsible for the flat blood-sugar curve. It should be noted, however, that these investigators did not think of making distinctions between various types of sugars and made no experiments with any carbohydrate other than glucose. It may be noted that the extreme difficulty of quantitative determination of carbohydrates in the feces casts doubt upon the conclusions of this work.

On the other hand, Ross,[504,505] in two papers in 1936, reported his belief that in celiac disease there was a defective absorption of carbohydrates from the intestine. Noting that in this condition a flat oral glucose tolerance test was associated with a high intravenous one, he found that intravenous glucose therapy brought the intravenous curves closer to normal. Commenting also upon the state of relative insensitivity to insulin in celiac disease, he went on to recommend total liver extracts as containing a factor capable of improving the glucose tolerance.

Badenock and Morris,[28] in the same year, reported, however, that celiac patients are more than normally sensitive to insulin, citing the fact that they showed a greater than normal reduction of blood sugar after injection of insulin. These investigators also reported other studies in carbohydrate metabolism. The height of the blood-sugar curve after ingestion of glucose, they stated, increased with age, the adult type of curve rarely being seen before the age of four. During the acute stage of celiac disease, they found the blood-sugar curve very flat, but during convalescence it approached normal, although there was frequently a lag. Moreover, only during convalescence was the height of the curve increased by an increase in the amount of glucose ingested. They reported, also, that during convalescent periods, the levulose curve was abnormally high, and that banana (rich in levulose) gave a higher curve than glucose. Badenock and Morris concluded that fermentation of carbohydrates was an important factor in the production of the flat curve after glucose ingestion, and in support of this view presented their results with banana and urea, neither of which is readily fermented. Finally, they pointed out that injection of anterior pituitary extract into celiac patients raised the level of the fasting blood-sugar, rendered the blood-sugar curve more normal in height and caused a slight improvement in the percentage absorption of fat but apparently had no effect on growth.

In 1942 Stannus [570] published a paper on sprue, which most writers, following Thaysen, have considered as probably identical with celiac disease. He noted that there was a primary loss of power to absorb glucose which resulted in the flat oral blood-sugar tolerance curve. He attributed this to failure of phosphorylation. Levulose, he pointed out, was utilized by the sprue patient in normal fashion, and this form of sugar did not require phosphorylation to be absorbed. Stannus believed that the failure of phosphorylation was the result of defective enzymic action which could be corrected by some factor of the vitamin B complex obtainable from crude liver extracts.

In one of her papers on the celiac syndrome, Andersen [13] reported on fecal excretion in cases of congenital pancreatic deficiency, a condition which she considers a distinct disease entity, quite different from celiac disease despite the fact that it reveals about the same clinical symptoms. She reported that carbohydrate was better utilized in the form of cereal starch than in the form of bananas, and that no great difference was observed in the utilization of bread and oatmeal as compared with that of potato and oatmeal. Starch and sugar, she stated, were clinically well tolerated. Despite these assurances, however, she recommended low-carbohydrate content in the diet. In her work on celiac disease, as distinguished by her from pancreatic deficiency, Andersen had at one time postulated a third ailment, distinct from both, which she termed starch intolerance. In her 1947 paper, however, she stated that experience had caused her to retract this hypothesis and to consider starch intolerance as a factor in celiac disease itself. She found inadequate digestion of starch in cases of all degrees of severity and at all stages, adding that there was clinical intolerance of starch in the diet, clinical response to elimination of starch from the diet, and an excess of starch in the feces when starch was fed. Andersen pointed out that examination of the feces for starch presented difficulties.

Scott [546] reported that it was well known that bananas were well tolerated in celiac disease and attributed this to the fact that most of the sugar in this fruit was in the form of invert sugar, a mixture of the monosaccharides, glucose and fructose. Cane sugar, on the other hand, was badly tolerated because it was a strongly dextrorotary sugar. He suggested that there may be an absence of the enzyme, invertase, in the intestine, or that the factor of absorption may be more important. But no conclusions were offered on these points.

In 1947 Emery [159,160] published two papers on carbohydrate metabolism. Making carefully controlled tests involving 13 cases of celiac disease, he found that oral glucose tolerance curves were flat and often showed periods of actual fall in blood-sugar level. The immediate fall in blood sugar due to insulin was normal, he found, but it did not regain its original level in the normal time. The relative failure of the blood sugar to rise after administration of insulin was not affected by adrenalin. This suggested that there was no deficiency of that hormone. But adrenalin, when not preceded by insulin, produced a rise in blood sugar less than normal. When oral glucose was given at the same time as adrenalin, there was an immediate and rapid rise in blood sugar level, as in normal subjects. Emery felt that his evidence showed that celiac patients could absorb glucose normally and utilize it normally, but that they lacked available glucose. He followed this work with a study of cold-sweating and concluded that cold-sweating in celiac children represented an acute carbohydrate deficiency independent of the blood-sugar level.

Somersalo [565] pointed out, in 1948, that his experiments indicated that intermediary carbohydrate metabolism in celiac patients was normal, but that absorption was impaired. Other findings, however, contradicted this thesis, and he concluded that the question was still unsolved.

In the same year, Ødegaard [485] reported on 27 patients who were given glucose tolerance tests 49 times. Great variations were found in the curves which varied greatly for the same patient and did not seem to depend on the severity of the disease. Ødegaard made tests to investigate the thesis that levulose is assimilated more easily than other carbohydrates in celiac disease. Finding the blood-sugar curves very low, he felt that levulose was not absorbed any more easily than other carbohydrates. It must be noted, however, that he used the blood-sugar curve as the only method of judging tolerance.

McLean and Sullivan,[380] in 1929, reporting on experiments with 14 patients, found that after ingestion of fructose and dextrose given in equal proportions, blood-sugar curves were obtained similar to those of normal children following the ingestion of dextrose. This, they believed, suggested a more normal metabolism of invert sugar and a possible explanation of the celiac patient's tolerance of bananas.

There is a long history of investigations along this line. Davison [127] suggested that in digestive disturbances in infants, especially in diarrhea and to a lesser extent in bacillary dysentery, the activity of the duodenal amylase and trypsin is decreased. Fleming and Hutchinson [185] found that in athreptic infants, proteins were best utilized and carbohydrates most poorly utilized. Crawford [120] seemed certain that the low blood-sugar curve of celiac disease must be due to delayed or defective absorption of carbohydrate from the intestine. Many authors have written about this problem, but the only conclusions that can be stated even tentatively from the history of the research are: (1) that the blood-sugar curve, although having some relation to celiac disease, is a secondary effect and cannot be used as a reliable test for assimilation of carbohydrates; (2) that clinical findings have shown that monosaccharides are tolerated in celiac disease while polysaccharides are not. In reviewing the literature it becomes apparent that no matter what viewpoint concerning the basic defect is taken—whether it be starch or fat intolerance—all authors exclude carbohydrates from the diet in treating the early stages of the disease.

MINERALS

Numerous studies have been made on the absorption of minerals in celiac disease. MacCrudden and Fales [355] reported that they found poor absorption from the intestine of nitrogen, sulphur, phosphorus, calcium and magnesium. Excretion of these substances in the urine was low. Excretion of calcium into the intestines was high, and complete balance experiments showed that while the other elements were retained, calcium was lost. This calcium loss, they felt, was responsible for failure to develop and grow normally. Bloch,[61] in 1927, attributed the occasional symptoms of tetany to insufficient absorption of calcium.

In 1928 Telfer [591] reported that in celiac disease he found that patients on a diet of fresh cow's milk retained very little of the bone-forming element. Retention of magnesia was not appreciably lessened, but that of iron was negative. Macrae and Morris [362] examined previous writers' views as to the efficacy of bile salts in aiding the absorption of fats and minerals. Although they could reach no conclusions, they felt that acid sodium phosphate had a good effect on both fat and mineral absorption because it altered the pH of the intestine.

Wampler and Forbes [639] reported in 1933 on a case of celiac disease which had continued for 8 years in which poor calcium and phosphorus balances were changed to strongly positive balances, with marked clinical improvement, with one month's treatment with liberal doses of vitamin D and increased calcium intake. Calcium retention was not only increased, but percentage retention was also increased. X-rays verified improvements in the long bones, but there was no improvement in growth. In 1939 Bassett and his colleagues [87,88] reported that levels of calcium and phosphorus intake, in the absence of vitamin D, failed to produce consistency positive balances of these elements.

The history of research in the relationships between minerals and celiac disease, while it is not extensive, goes back a long way. In 1917 Holt, Sr., and his co-workers [266] showed a very striking loss in mineral salts in celiac disease; and all later research has tended to substantiate this observation. There is, now, quite general agreement that calcium metabolism is dependent on the general metabolic picture in celiac disease, that calcium is absorbed and utilized properly with sufficient vitamin D, which in turn is somewhat dependent for its efficacy on the presence of a certain amount of fat in the diet.

A number of writers, in discussing mineral metabolism, have pointed out that during the severe untreated phase, when steatorrhea is present, the steatorrhea, per se, can be blamed for faulty mineral absorption, since, during this phase, the fats are split normally, and the resultant fatty acids form insoluble soaps with calcium, phosphorus, etc., thus interfering with the absorption of these mineral elements, thus causing the osteoporosis so frequently observed in this phase of the disease. By the same token, the fat-soluble vitamins are not absorbed, resulting in the observed low vitamin A tolerance curves.

VITAMINS

Avitaminosis was, for some time, considered among other etiologic factors in connection with celiac disease. As a matter of fact, the symptoms of severe celiac disease were thought to be due to an avitaminosis. Although this theory was discarded some time ago, every writer on the subject has recognized the importance of vitamins in the therapy of celiac disease. Most of the work was done on vitamins A and D, but more recent research has concentrated on the role of the B complex in the disease.

In 1928, Bloch [61] considered vitamin C as a factor. This was because he considered the reported success of the use of bananas to indicate a lack of vitamin C which the fruit furnished. Since the proponents of the banana diet did not consider the vitamin C content of the fruit to be the important factor in its efficacy in treating celiac disease, it is not surprising that Bloch obtained no positive findings to support his theory. Furthermore, if the rest of his diet were improper, the mere inclusion of banana would not bring about clinical improvement. Bloch finally concluded that infantilism is not due to an avitaminosis.

The report of Wampler and Forbes [639] in 1933, which has been cited previously, noted the beneficial effects of liberal doses of vitamin D along with increased calcium intake, but no data on the diet were supplied.

In 1936 Fridericksen [200] reported on resorption of vitamin A in a case of celiac disease. Using a special eye examination to determine the degree of A hypovitaminosis, he found a fairly severe condition. The vitamin A contained in sweet milk, mashed carrots, spinach and in a concentrated vitamin A preparation was not resorbed. After administration of mother's milk, however, he found that the eye test showed a normal reaction. May and McCreary,[373] in 1941, studied vitamin A absorption in 23 infants with celiac disease. They found that a low rise in the level of vitamin A in the blood during vitamin A absorption tests was a consistent feature of celiac disease. Since this same reaction occurs in numerous conditions, the test is of no diagnostic value, but it might be helpful, they felt, in following clinical recovery from the disease. Gonce,[220] too, noted the same deficiency of vitamin A absorption and said that it was about ten per cent of normal.

Writing of pancreatic insufficiency presenting the celiac syndrome in 1943, Farber [178] postulated three possible causes for the condition, one of which was vitamin A deficiency. He noted Andersen's finding of some evidence of vitamin A deficiency upon histologic examination of certain organs in 23 per cent of the cases studied or collected. Farber himself found it less frequently. He concluded that deficiency of vitamin A was only one of the complications of the disease and not of primary etiologic significance.

Numerous observers have noted that most of the symptoms of the critical period of celiac disease disappear with remarkable rapidity under appropriate dietary and vitamin therapy, and they agreed that there was strong evidence to indicate that the critical period represented a multiple deficiency state which was almost always reversible under proper treatment. They noted, also, that steatorrhea was associated with poor absorption of vitamin A and supported the earlier findings of May and McCreary that intensive therapy with vitamin B complex and liver concentrates restored the normal vitamin A absorption curve within a short period.

In 1949 Danielson et al.[125] made tests to determine the absorption of vitamin A from oily and aqueous media in infants and children suffering from conditions presenting the celiac syndrome. They made a distinction between those considered to have cystic fibrosis of the pancreas and those with celiac disease. Patients with cystic fibrosis of the pancreas, they stated, could absorb vitamin A acetate and vitamin A alcohol when administered in an aqueous dispersion. The celiac patients absorbed vitamin A only slightly better from an aqueous dispersion of the alcohol than from an oily concentrate of the naturally occurring esters. Recent clinical evidence shows that this does not hold true, the aqueous dispersion being far superior, and ordinary cod-liver oil being borne poorly.

Lewy,[346] in 1940, pointed out that all known fractions of the vitamin B complex act as enzymes and play an important role in the carbohydrate metabolism of plants and animals. He further noted that there is evidence that incomplete combustion of fat is a consequence of carbohydrate deficiency. Molnar and Noszko [410] bore this out, contending that vitamin B_1 was indispensable in the regulation of carbohydrate metabolism, and Tislowitz [608] came to a similar conclusion.

The sum total of recent research tends to support the almost universally recognized use of supplementary vitamins A and D in treating celiac disease. Most discussion now centers about the B complex in connection with the use of liver extracts. There is agreement, too, that, although the role of vitamins is important, it is not etiologically fundamental. Certainly, vitamin B may help in the neurologic aspects of the disease.

10

Digestive Juices, Enzymes, etc.

Since celiac disease is a disturbance of the digestive tract, it was only natural to search for the etiology of the condition in some deficiency of the digestive juices or enzymes. Over the years numerous deficiencies have been reported; however, almost as many reports have indicated that no deficiencies existed. Only in the case of the pancreatic enzymes has any group of findings led to a widely accepted conclusion. While such enzymes were not found to be lacking in even a majority of cases, their deficiency was reported with sufficient regularity to suggest to numerous investigators that two separate conditions displaying the celiac syndrome existed: one which should be called celiac disease; the other, cystic fibrosis of the pancreas or congenital pancreatic insufficiency. It will perhaps be best to outline work in other fields first and then return to the question of the pancreatic enzymes, a subject about which there is much current writing.

Cheadle [104] was the first to suggest that the symptoms of celiac disease were caused by an absence of bile. He even felt that the name, acholia, was appropriate. But the chief basis of his belief was the pale color of the stools, and upon postmortem he was unable to find any pathology in either the liver or the pancreas. Mumford,[422] in 1908, reported on several cases apparently lacking bile in the feces. This also indicated to him that fats were not being assimilated properly.

Later, attention turned from bile to bile salts. Miller,[889] in 1920, found that there was no defect in fat splitting, but that the administration of bile salts improved it somewhat.

He could find no evidence pointing to pancreatic insufficiency in celiac disease. In 1923 Miller and Perkins [401] concluded that the pale color of the typical celiac stool was not due to an absence of bile pigment but to a masking of the pigment by an excess of fatty acid crystals. Lehndorff and Mautner [339] reported alteration in the production of bile and difficulty with the pancreatic juices, but they felt that neither condition was of primary importance.

Recognizing the general but unsubstantiated view that some digestive secretion failed in celiac disease, Kundratitz [324] examined the duodenal juices of his two cases and found them normal. He added, further, that the cases of Göttche showed the same normalcy. Bischoff,[55] in 1930, reported definite clinical improvement on administration of bile salts orally, but he believed that no conclusions could be drawn from this evidence alone. Macrae and Morris [862] went more thoroughly into the question of bile salts, reporting on the work of others in the field, including Fanconi's failure to achieve clinical improvement through administration of bile salts. Their own results were conflicting, since they noted both increased and decreased fat and mineral absorption after use of bile salts. In one case, however, they found that bile salts caused a more normal carbohydrate metabolism. They pointed out also that in celiac disease the metabolic picture was vastly different from that of such conditions as atresia of the bile duct where there was complete absence of bile. This indicated, they felt, that there was no lack of bile in celiac disease. Subsequent investigators have verified this finding. Many have found no deficiency of any kind in digestive juices or enzymes, among them Gonce,[220] who in 1942 reported that he found no evidence to indicate anything but normal enzymatic activity. Scott's [646] suggestion that there was a lack of invertase was a deduction rather than the result of actual chemical analysis. No current writer seems to consider the possible lack of bile salts as an important factor in celiac disease.

Almost the same conclusion has been reached concerning the possibility of deficiency of hydrochloric acid. Although some investigators even today report finding hypoacidity in some cases, this condition is not a primary cause of difficulty. Even among earlier writers, it never loomed as large potentially as did bile and bile salts. In 1922 Marriott [370] reported on two cases of celiac disease in which examination of the stomach contents at the height of the illness revealed almost complete absence of hydrochloric acid. He recommended that the diet be one that did not tend to neutralize the acid, and he also suggested the administration of 5 or 10 cc. of normal hydrochloric acid before feeding. He pointed out, however, that the latter treatment must not be continued for more than a few days at a time. In their series of 7 cases, Snell and Camp [562] found a marked deficiency of hydrochloric acid in the gastric juice. This deficiency was overcome as the general condition improved. Parsons [446] stated that achlorhydria was not uncommon in celiac disease, but he found that free acid could be obtained in response to histamine. In 1935 Ogilvie [436] studied the gastric secretions of 17 celiac children and compared them with normal children of the same age range. She found that in every case of celiac disease there was impaired secretion of hydrochloric acid, but that true achlorhydria did not exist. There was no diminution of peptic activity, but a slight prolongation in emptying time. She found that secretion of free hydrochloric acid increased as the patient improved. However, so many writers have reported finding no abnormality in gastric secretions that the current consensus is probably expressed by the statement that sometimes gastric hypoacidity may be found. It is certainly not a primary factor in celiac disease.

By far the greatest amount of work in connection with digestive juices in celiac disease has been concerned with the pancreatic enzymes and findings of pathology in the pancreas. From the earliest days there have been many cases in which deficient pancreatic function was reported; so many, in fact, that some writers began to feel that they were not dealing here with the same kind of contradictory findings reported about most of the other symptoms and pathologic conditions of celiac disease. Here, they felt, the contradictions meant that there were two separate disease entities. It is surprising, in some ways, that this notion of a separate disease should have suggested itself in connection with the pancreas. Of course, the same thing held true, at one time or another, about other symptoms of celiac disease. It has been noted that a few writers, especially Fanconi,[165] made a distinction between celiac disease and intestinal infantilism. But this view did not persist or gain widespread acceptance. For a time Andersen thought that starch intolerance was a disease condition distinct from celiac disease or pancreatic insufficiency. But she later reconsidered this idea and lumped starch intolerance with celiac disease. But she did not alter her views about the distinction that she made between celiac disease and cystic fibrosis of the pancreas. The majority of writers today accept this distinction, and the standard textbooks usually treat celiac disease and pancreatic insufficiency as two separate conditions presenting almost the same set of symptoms. It is likely that this thesis gained wide acceptance at a time when most writers felt that celiac disease did not begin until the first year of life, more commonly in the second year. Yet they found some cases presenting this syndrome from birth, and in such cases there was pathology in the pancreas. Therefore, the idea very naturally presented itself that the pancreatic condition was congenital and thus different from celiac disease. Apparently, it did not occur to most writers that they were failing to recognize celiac disease in its early mild phases and that they were therefore assuming that it did not start until after the first year of life. Those cases that were recognized from birth were apt to be severe ones, and in very severe cases pancreatic function may be altered and the pancreas itself show drastic pathologic changes. By the time it was generally recognized that celiac disease could and did occur from birth, the idea of a separate disease entity involving the pancreas was firmly entrenched in the minds of most pediatricians. They will agree that celiac disease may or may not show steatorrhea (once considered the primary symptom), that it may show diarrhea or constipation, that it may come on suddenly or slowly, that it may show normal hydrochloric acid or achlorhydria, that it may be accompanied by tetany, anemia, osteoporosis, edema, enlarged heart, or by none of these complications, that pathology may be found in numerous organs or may not be found at all. In other words, they will agree that almost every symptom and condition of celiac disease found in most cases will be found not to exist in some cases. And, contrariwise, that some symptoms and pathologic conditions are found in celiac disease in some cases but not in the majority of cases.

When they come to the subject of the pancreas, however, they alter their general view about the variability in incidence and degree of all symptoms in celiac disease. They find pancreatic insufficiency in numerous cases, of course, but they do not state that here, once again, is a condition which is found only sometimes in celiac disease. They say instead that this is not celiac disease at all but a separate disease entity. This new disease and celiac disease may show the same symptoms and may respond to a similar treatment but according to this view they are nevertheless separate diseases.

Bramwell's case, reported originally in 1902 [72] and a number of times thereafter (although always the same case), was doubtless one in which there was pancreatic insufficiency. At least, the patient improved considerably on administration of pancreatic extract. Other writers have noted what they considered definite evidence of deficient pancreatic activity in numerous cases. In 1920 Moorhead [416] reported on two cases, one of which showed a normal pancreas at postmortem. The second responded so well to treatment with liquor pancreaticus, holadin and bile salts capsules, plus a special diet, that Moorhead felt that it was a case of pancreatic infantilism similar to that reported by Bramwell. Marriott [370] commented on the fact that in celiac disease there was sometimes a slight atrophy of the pancreas, but that it was only one of several pathologic conditions occasionally present.

Lehndorff and Mautner [321] noted difficulties with functions of the pancreas and the liver in celiac disease, but felt that they were secondary. They also found common pathologic changes in the pancreas, with a definite increase in the interlobular connective tissue, chiefly that surrounding the excretory ducts. But this was only part of a general pathologic picture found on postmortem in severe cases of celiac disease. In 1930 Parsons [445] wrote that in 8 cases pancreatic juice obtained by duodenal intubation showed that lipase was present in normal amounts. These cases were apparently those of celiac disease in the strictest sense rather than those of cystic fibrosis of the pancreas. In the light of recent investigation concerning duodenal enzymes, the value of duodenal lipase determinations has been shown to be doubtful.

Working on the theory that defective functioning of the pancreas might be the cause of celiac disease, Greenberg,[227] in 1933, tried to induce the disease experimentally in young animals. In rats, total elimination of the external pancreatic secretion was found to be anatomically impractical because the pancreas drains into the bile duct through from 3 to 5 main ducts and innumerable tiny ones. After ligation of the main ducts in the rat, Greenberg found that the animal showed no significant changes in weight, growth, health, or digestion except for a slight increase in the percentage of fat excreted in the stools. Autopsies showed a considerable amount of normal pancreatic tissue remaining.

Greenberg found that he could exclude the pancreatic juice completely in the cat by ligating the main and the accessory ducts. This caused an immediate and continued loss of weight, the passage of from 3 to 4 times the normal quantity of stools, an almost complete failure of fat absorption, a marked decline in nitrogen absorption, and an extreme emaciation leading to death. At autopsy the pancreas was found to be entirely lacking in normal acinar tissue. In some cases, when death did not result from the above symptoms, autopsies showed some normal pancreatic tissue remaining. A fraction of normal pancreas was apparently adequate to maintain growth and health. Greenberg concluded that complete exclusion of pancreatic secretions from the intestine brought about a condition comparable with that of pancreatic insufficiency in man. He suggested that dysfunction of one or two of the pancreatic enzymes might produce the condition known as celiac disease. On the other hand, it is well known that surgical exclusion of pancreatic exocrine secretions from the intestine in humans does not always result in diarrhea, emaciation, etc. Thaysen [598] worked to investigate the theory that some fatty diarrhea was of pancreatic origin, while another type did not involve the pancreas. Anderson and Lyall,[19] in 1933, conducted a series of tests along this line, working chiefly with nitrogen metabolism. Seeking for some method of differential diagnosis, they put a patient on a fat-deficient diet, then measured the nitrogen and the fat content of the stool. If the fecal nitrogen remained high, they concluded that this was an indication of pancreatogenous fatty diarrhea. If the nitrogen content was less than 3 Gm. daily, they felt that this indicated idiopathic steatorrhea without pancreatic damage. Although this work was done on adults, it may well be that the conditions they dealt with were an adult form of celiac disease.

In 1938 Harper [246] reported on 8 cases of children showing the usual celiac symptoms. In an effort to differentiate between celiac disease and what he called congenital steatorrhea, Harper listed several differences. In congenital steatorrhea, he said, symptoms were present from birth, whereas in celiac disease they appeared at from 9 months to 2 years of age. It is now generally recognized, of course, that celiac disease may exist from birth. Harper stated that there was oil in the stools in congenital steatorrhea but not in celiac disease. Other writers have reported contradictory findings, and many writers now agree that steatorrhea itself is not even an essential in celiac disease. In both conditions, Harper said, there was high fecal fat, but he maintained that in congenital steatorrhea it was unsplit. Later writers found great variations in the fats in the stools. Harper found the glucose tolerance curve high in congenital steatorrhea, flat in celiac disease, and reported postmortem findings of pancreatic lesions in the first condition with no such lesions in the second. However, many writers have reported some pathology in the pancreas in numerous cases of celiac disease, although this is far from a universal finding.

Sidney Farber,[178-181] alone and with co-workers, published a series of interesting papers on pancreatic insufficiency and the celiac syndrome. In 1941 he reported on 50 determinations of pancreatic enzymes (trypsin, amylase, lipase) in three types of children—normal, those suffering from celiac disease, and those with the pancreatic fibrosis variation of the celiac syndrome. In the children with celiac disease, all pancreatic enzymes were well within the normal range. They were greatly reduced or absent in those who were found at autopsy to have had pancreatic fibrosis. In one of these, alterations were confined to the acini, and there was no obstruction in the larger ducts. He concluded that pancreatic enzymes may be abnormally low even before gross obstruction of the ducts has occurred. Determination of the pancreatic enzymes in the duodenal contents, Farber felt, was the only positive diagnostic device to differentiate between celiac disease and pancreatic fibrosis.

In 1943 Farber et al. reported on 150 determinations of pancreatic enzyme activity. They found pancreatic achylia to be a constant finding in patients in whom postmortem examination revealed obstructive changes in the duct-acinar system of the pancreas. But patients with celiac disease showed no pancreatic achylia. Farber felt that no diagnosis of celiac disease, idiopathic steatorrhea, nontropical sprue, pancreatic fibrosis, or other similar disease should be considered final until pancreatic enzyme activity had been measured.

In the same year, in another paper, Farber listed the various conditions that could cause pancreatic achylia and then examined three theories of the cause of the condition as associated with the celiac syndrome. He felt that vitamin A deficiency and a filterable virus could not easily be supported as the causes. This led him to investigate more thoroughly the thesis put forth by Blackfan [58] that there was production of an abnormal pancreatic secretion. Study of 87 cases of advanced pancreatic lesion and about 350 cases in early stages supported the hypothesis that there was a physically altered pancreatic secretion which caused intrinsic obstruction in the acini and the small ducts, leading finally to a dilation and an obstruction of the larger ducts. Atrophy of the acinar structures followed, and condensation of the connective-tissue framework combined with an ingrowth of new fibrous tissue.

Further support was offered, Farber felt, by the observation that the fully developed clinical picture of the celiac syndrome may exist and the pancreatic enzymes in the duodenal contents may be reduced markedly even when the sole lesion in the pancreas consists of inspissation of secretion in the acini and small ducts with no evidence of atrophy of the parenchyma, fibrosis, or dilation of the large ducts. He found further evidence of the abnormality of the pancreatic secretion in the gross appearance of the scanty, extremely thick and viscid pancreatic juice obtained in the duodenal contents contrasted with the thin, watery pancreatic juice from normal infants or from those suffering from "true" celiac disease. Farber pointed out further that inspissation of secretions and dilatation of glandular structure of the same general character were also found at autopsy in the glands of the trachea, bronchi, esophagus, duodenum, gallbladder and intestinal tract. He concluded that his findings suggested that the inspissation of altered secretions in the pancreatic acini was only a part of a generalized disorder of secretory mechanisms, involving many glandular structures but exerting its greatest effect on the pancreas. In experiments on kittens he found it possible to produce similar conditions by the administration of sympatheticomimetic drugs (Pilocarpine and acetylmethylcholine). The cause of the disturbance of the secretory mechanism remained to be demonstrated, Farber felt.

Going further in the same line of thought, Farber expressed his belief in 1943 that the pancreatic condition on which he had been working was really a part of a systemic disease. Many authors, he felt, had neglected the respiratory and other changes associated with the pancreatic damage. The next year he suggested that the systemic nature of this condition indicated hopeful lines of investigation into the nervous control of the secretion of the pancreatic and the mucus glands. In all of his work Farber was emphatic in making a clear distinction between pancreatic fibrosis and "true" celiac disease, and his views carried great weight.

Philipsborn et al.,[456] in 1945, described a method by which they distinguished between cystic fibrosis of the pancreas and celiac disease by analyzing the enzymatic activity of duodenal contents and by noting the volumetric responses of the pancreas to secretin or $N/10$ HCl. Their conclusion was essentially the same as that of others working in the field, that enzymatic activity in pancreatic fibrosis was markedly diminished, while that in celiac disease was normal or nearly so. In 1948 Baggenstoss[29] suggested that the absence of pancreatic juice was the result of an intrinsic obstruction secondary to congenital deficiency of secretion.

In a series of papers on the celiac syndrome Andersen and her co workers [8-17] published material of great influence on all physicians interested in celiac disease and related conditions. In the first of these she tested methods of examining fecal fat, pointing out that changes in lipid partition sometimes occur in samples of stools as ordinarily collected, thus giving unreliable figures. Some of the earlier work on fat excretion done by earlier investigators may well have contained serious errors due to the unreliable methods of measurement. In her next paper she reported statistics on excretion of fecal fat by patients of various ages with congenital pancreatic deficiency while on normal diet. Stools were usually formed and normal in appearance but of penetrating odor, and the fat was excessive for all patients. The results of administration of pancreatin were variable, but amounts of fecal fat and total fecal excretion were usually reduced. She then made a series of studies to determine the best diet, and in the next paper expanded on that diet and discussed prognosis. The fourth paper in the series, with Di Sant'Agnese, dealt with the respiratory infections associated with cystic fibrosis of the pancreas. The next paper, with Hodges, treated of the genetics of pancreatic fibrosis. The authors felt that the incidence of the condition suggested that it was a relatively infrequent hereditary trait which required more than one factor for its expression. The lesion of the pancreas, they stated, was not a malformation in the true sense, but appeared in the latter part of pregnancy, probably from an abnormality of the acinar secretion. They found a comparable disturbance in the liver, the gallbladder and the intestines, agreeing in large measure with Farber. They felt, however, that the pulmonary lesion began after birth and was primarily the result of nutritional deficiency.

In 1947 Andersen published a long paper attempting to find a way to separate patients presenting the celiac syndrome into groups on the basis of etiology and pathogenesis. Defining celiac disease, she then reported on 83 cases that fit the definition. On these cases, she did an assay of pancreatic enzymes and a chemical analysis of fecal fat. She eliminated cases of what she termed cystic fibrosis of the pancreas on the basis of failure to demonstrate normal levels of trypsin in the duodenal juice. In the celiac cases, she reported normal concentration of lipase in the duodenal juice. She stressed the fact that she commonly found pancreatic amylase absent or present only in small quantities. This finding she coupled with the observation that there was clinical intolerance to starch in the diet, clinical response to elimination of starch from the diet, and an excess of starch in the feces when starch was fed.

She pointed out, however, that there were difficulties in assaying amylase in the duodenal juice. First, there was the frequent admixture of gastric juice with the duodenal contents resulting in varying degrees of dilution of the pancreatic juice. Second, there was the frequent occurrence of gastric hypoacidity in patients with celiac disease, resulting in the presence of amylase from swallowed saliva in the gastric juices. Third, there was the fact that amylase was normally absent from the duodenal juice in the neonatal period, and that the normal ratio of amylase to trypsin in the second half of the first year was on the order of 50 per cent, while after one year of age it ranged between 50 and 150 per cent. Thus Andersen concluded that the determination of amylase concentration could not be used to substantiate the diagnosis in infants under 6 months of age.

Investigations of the role of digestive enzymes in the etiology of celiac disease have been carried on now for many years. As far back as 1919 Passini [450] pointed to the pancreas as a possible cause for the condition. Other authors have discussed other organs and their possible connection with the disease. Much attention has been given to the role of the liver. Various authors have investigated the other organs of the digestive system and their secretions. There can be no doubt that deficiency of the digestive juices is not uncommon in celiac disease. Most important, apparently, is the dysfunction or altered structure of the pancreatic enzymes. There may be some validity in the distinction between celiac disease and cystic fibrosis of the pancreas, although the evidence is inconclusive. That the distinction may be made by complex tests may be true, but, as Comfort and his co-workers [114] point out in a recent paper, the differentiation may be accomplished by clinical data and by less expensive and less time-consuming methods.

11

Endocrine System

Many writers on celiac disease have suggested that the basic cause of the ailment may lie in the endocrine system, but little pathologic evidence to support this hypothesis has been reported. Hess and Saphir [257] said that the thymus, the thyroid, and the suprarenals showed no gross or histologic changes. Mader,[364] in 1926, suggested that the condition was due to a disordered vegetative nervous system caused, in turn, by some defect in the hormonal system. Lehndorff and Mautner [339] summed up the literature in their monograph and found no reported evidence of thyroid insufficiency. As in all other cases of starvation, the thymus was atrophied. There had been no studies of the parathyroid. Some authors had observed alterations in the pituitary gland. In general it was shown that while there was difficulty with all the glands of internal secretion in celiac disease, there was no indication that these disorders were anything but secondary in nature.

In a report on a case of presumed celiac disease in 1932, De Ville and Myers [136] attributed the cause of the delay in development to hypofunction of the thyroid. Nevertheless, they could not completely exclude achondroplasia as the real condition. In any event, it was an unusual case. Badenock and Morris,[28] in 1936, stated that injection of anterior pituitary extract into patients with celiac disease raised the level of the fasting blood sugar, rendered the blood-sugar curve more normal in height, and caused a slight improvement in the percentage absorption of fat but did not seem to have any effect on growth. Verzar [625] looked elsewhere in the endocrine system and, as a result of long studies, reported in 1937 that celiac disease and nontropical sprue should be looked upon as possible adrenocortical disturbances of absorption. He felt that due to insufficient production of the adrenal cortical hormone, there was a basic disturbance in the special activity process in the intestinal mucosa. His patients responded well to liver extract, he reported, and to such yeast extracts as contain undestroyed flavinphosphoric acid. Adrenocortical hormone in quantities, he suggested, should be expected to be effective. Although Verzar showed that adrenalectomy in young animals produced symptoms very much like those of celiac disease, there were no other evidences of an adrenal disturbance such as would be expected if the basic cause of celiac disease lay in that gland.

Johnston and Howard [292] presented the thesis in 1949 that celiac disease was perhaps a condition having multiple causes, in which thyroid deficiency was a conditioning factor. They noted that arrested growth usually had been attributed to the fecal losses in the disease rather than to its status as an integral part of the metabolic difficulty. In many of their cases digestive symptoms appeared later than would explain the retardation of bone age, and the commonest time of appearance of bowel symptoms coincided with a decelerating phase and a falling rate of metabolism. Hypothyroidism and the celiac syndrome, they pointed out, have in common abnormalities in the metabolism of protein, fat, carbohydrate and calcium and in gastro-intestinal motility. The flat oral tolerance curve of the celiac is also seen in the hypothyroid. The failure to absorb glucose is seen not only in celiac disease but in the thyroidectomized animal. Failure to retain calcium was significant, too, as the authors had shown in a previous study that normal retention of calcium could be expected only with a normal level of thyroid activity.

Except for the abnormal stools, Johnston and Howard stated, there were many significant duplications of symptoms in celiac disease and hypothyroidism. They suggested that some infants might have their digestive disorders precipitated by infection, emotion, or allergy, but that the development of the disorders is conditioned by an underlying thyroid deficiency. Complementing the high protein diet with thyroid should, they thought, notably shorten the duration of the mild cases and correct an otherwise irreplaceable deficiency in the severe cases. In their treatment the authors found this to be true. In 18 cases the average time before cessation of symptoms was 9 months instead of the 17 months that elapsed in those treated with proper diet but without supplementary thyroid. Five children were symptom-free in less than 2 months.

Other very interesting work has been done on the role of the endocrine system in celiac disease. Laszt and Verzar [334] showed that after extirpation of the adrenal gland, absorption of fat is greatly hindered and that metabolism of sugar and salt is also severely altered. The great amount of work done in recent years on the effects of adrenal-cortical substances has shown that various steroids isolated from the adrenal cortex exhibit striking differences in their effect on carbohydrate and electrolyte metabolism. Loeschke [350] believes that, although there is manifest atrophy of the glands of inner secretion in celiac disease, this manifestation is secondary, and the theory that the disorder is primarily one of glandular origin is untenable.

Although very little significant work has been reported recently in the field of the connection of endocrinology and celiac disease, many avenues of investigation reveal themselves as well worthy of being followed. Even if the endocrine system does not finally disclose the origin of celiac disease, it may well tell us much more about the condition than we now know.

12

Nervous System and Psychological Considerations

As early as 1889 Gibbons [210] suggested the nervous system as the clue to celiac disease. Many others, including Cheadle,[104] Czerny,[124] and Kleinschmidt [313] were inclined to agree. Herter stated that various minor signs of nervous instability were found in cases of intestinal infantilism. He ascribed the intoxication which is so prominent a feature of the disease to the action of the putrefactive products of intestinal origin upon the central nervous system and muscles.

In 1925 Freise and Jahr [197] concluded, as a result of studying two cases, that celiac disease was a vegetative neurosis which was only a portion of a constitutional weakness of the entire nervous system. They felt that the common symptoms of celiac disease were brought about by an increased motility of the stomach and the small intestine and offered clinical and roentgenologic evidence to support their contention. They quieted portions of the digestive tract with atropin or opium and found that metabolism came close to normal and that the stools and the general condition improved. Six years later Freise and Walenta [198] reported on animal experiments to verify these hypotheses. Feeling that the immediate cause of hypermotility was either a lowered tonus of the splanchnic nerve or an elevated tonus of the vagus nerve, they severed the former in dogs and in young swine. As a result, symptoms tallying closely with the most common ones of celiac disease were produced—chronic diarrhea with voluminous fatty stools, increased motility of the gut, enlarged abdomen and arrested development.

From Gibbons on, various investigators have given more or less emphasis to the psychoneuropathology of celiac disease. Hablützel-Weber [238] maintained that 4 of his cases showed signs of neuropathology. Mader [364] found some weakness of the nervous system as a hereditary factor in most of his cases. Lehndorff and Mautner, [339] although they admitted the possibility of psychoneuropathology, felt that the evidence was insufficient. Moorhead, [416] in postmortem study, found changes in the structure of the pituitary gland. Allibone [5] observed tiny patches of demyelization of the posterior columns of the spinal cord. Schiff [533] placed more emphasis on this possibility in arriving at an etiology of the disease than did most other students of the illness. DeTakats and Cuthbert [134] showed that the experimental removal of the celiac ganglion causes clear changes in sugar metabolism. Kundratitz [324] believed that there was neuropathology, especially of the vegetative system. Hassmann [248] asserted that there were evidences of neuropathology in all his cases. Wade [637] suggests that the cause of celiac disease ultimately may be found in a general smooth muscle dystrophy or in a disturbance of innervation in the sympathetic nervous system. Czerny and Keller [124] feel that the etiology rests solely on neuropathology. Kleinschmidt [313] also believes that the disease is primarily neurogenic. Hurst [279] believes that a dysfunction in Meissner's plexus may be responsible for the ailment. Farber [179] feels that the cause of the disease ultimately may be found in the nervous system and suggests that further research on etiology should be directed toward the nervous control of secretion of the pancreatic and mucous glands.

Many authors have suggested the possible psychogenesis of celiac disease or at least the important role of the emotions in the condition. Kleinschmidt, [313] Hablützel-Weber, [238] Schiff, [533] Czerny and Keller, [124] Andersen, [11] Johnston and

Howard,[292] and others have emphasized the psychological aspects of the disease, and some writers are ready to name the psychological aberration as an etiologic factor of celiac disease.

Lovell observed fibrosis of the pancreas or focal pancreatic necrosis in patients with involutional melancholia and later published observations in which anxiety as a psychotic symptom was associated with pathologic evidence of pancreatic disease. He suggested that an alteration in the viscosity of the serum may precipitate the pancreatic lesions and cerebral edema, which he considered as the basis for the mental symptoms. In the blood-sugar studies that Drury [143] and Farran-Ridge performed on patients showing confusion and melancholia, they demonstrated that a disturbed sugar metabolism was common. They also described 5 cases of anxiety syndrome in which death was due to pancreatitis. Mann,[367] also, found abnormal blood-sugar curves in a large series of patients showing melancholia or anxiety neurosis. Lups,[352] too, points out that the brain participates in the regulation of carbohydrate metabolism and, although he points out that the mechanism of this regulation is not yet understood, he maintains that disturbances in carbohydrate metabolism do not always arise from anatomic lesions in the mesodiencephalon. In certain cases he believes that the whole clinical picture indicates a functional weakness of particular regions of the brain.

Although there is too little evidence to point to neurogenic or psychogenic factors as the cause of celiac disease, and although we feel that the emotional disturbances associated with the disease are secondary rather than primary, we feel that with the increasing evidence of the determining role of the emotions in so many diseases formerly considered entirely physiological, it would seem that the psychic field should be investigated thoroughly.

13

Allergy

In 1942 Kunstadter [325] suggested that some conditions showing the celiac syndrome and heretofore considered as celiac disease in reality might be cases of gastro-intestinal allergy. He reported on 3 cases of the celiac syndrome that gave many evidences that they might be the result of food allergy. In 2 of the 3 there was a family history of allergy, and these 2 also showed other manifestations of allergy: rhinorrhea and eczema in one, and eczema in the other. All 3 infants had multiple food allergies, as evidenced either by trial and error methods or by skin testing. Not one could tolerate cow's milk, which was the most serious offender. Its elimination from the diet resulted in a cessation of the diarrhea in all 3 cases.

Two of the cases had shown negative cutaneous and intra-cutaneous tests to milk, a finding which brought up the question, Kunstadter stated, of the value of skin-testing in infants, who often showed contradictory responses. He suggested, however, that gastro-intestinal allergy be considered in all cases that did not respond favorably to the so-called celiac diet. In such cases he recommends eliminating milk and other possible allergens, but since almost all celiac diets now omit cow's milk and advise some kind of protein milk, Kunstadter's suggestions are not very pertinent. Cow's milk is not well tolerated in celiac disease, except as protein milk, entirely apart from any consideration of allergy.

McKhann and his co-workers [379] published a paper in 1943 on the possible association of gastro-intestinal allergy with celiac disease, in which they cited Kunstadter as well as

Riley [492] who, in 1939, had described celiac symptomatology associated with eczema. These authors stated that their observations tended to confirm the latter association, citing three types of cases. First, there was celiac cases which gave some evidence of allergy through scratch or intradermal sensitization tests. Kunstadter, however, had already called such tests unreliable in children. McKhann and his colleagues also pointed out that some outspoken cases of gastro-intestinal allergy showed symptoms very close to those of celiac disease. Finally, in certain other types of allergic conditions, they observed interference with absorption of food substances similar to that which occurs in celiac disease. They concluded that, although an association might exist between allergy and the celiac syndrome, it was possible that the symptomatology of gastro-intestinal allergy might simulate that of celiac disease, even when the latter diagnosis was finally ruled out.

In 1949 Bloch [63] also reported that celiac disease was an allergic response in which the chief offender was cow's milk. He suggested that, in addition to all the other tests for allergy, an examination of a clear particle of mucus from the feces to disclose the presence of eosinophils.

One finds evidence of allergy among celiac patients in the same proportion as in the general population, and most writers today agree that there is probably no association between the two conditions. Johnston and Howard,[292] it has already been noted, suggested allergy among other disturbances as a possible precipitating factor in celiac disease, the development of which was conditioned by hypothyroidism. But no evidence has been adduced up to this time which is sufficient to show conclusively that celiac disease is an allergic response.

14

Diagnosis

The diagnosis of celiac disease still must be based on the same obscure data which existed when Gee first described the condition over 60 years ago. At different periods, different symptoms have been held to be of highest importance, each one of them later being relegated, by some writer or another, to a relatively minor position. Thus, at one time, fatty stools were supposed to be pathognomic. Later evidence, however, showed that this symptom appeared prominently in other diseases that were completely unrelated to celiac disease. A flat blood-sugar curve was given great weight for a while, but now it is known to have only corroborative value in diagnosis. Infantilism, too, once held to be pathognomic, is now known to be present in only a minor percentage of cases. Even the classical bulging belly and flat buttocks are no longer accepted as pathognomic for celiac disease. Nevertheless, each of the diagnostic criteria presented by writers on celiac disease has its value in arriving at a diagnosis of the condition.

Perhaps the three most valuable descriptions of the diagnostic features of celiac disease have been given by Gee,[205] Herter,[253] and Howland.[272] Howland's description, especially, is faultless and clear.

Gee said:

There is a kind of chronic indigestion which is met with in persons of all ages, yet is especially apt to affect children between one and five years of age. Signs of the disease are yielded by the feces; being loose, not formed, but not watery; more bulky than the food taken would seem to account for; pale in color, as if devoid of bile; yeasty, frothy, an appearance due to fermentation; stinking, stench often very great, the food having undergone putrefaction rather than concoction.

Herter described the disease as being presented usually between the ages of 4 and 8 after the patient had been ill for a year. There are pronounced irregularities of the intestinal tract, disturbed nutrition, loss of weight alternating with periods of improvement and gain, ultimately culminating in completely arrested development. In addition to the intestinal flora of a definite type which he observed in celiac disease, Herter listed other symptoms such as marked abdominal distention; maintenance of mental powers despite the arrested bodily development; marked anemia; rapid fatigability; nervous irritability; various obtrusive irregularities of the intestinal tract such as diarrhea, soft stools, frequent movements, steatorrhea, and soap and fatty acid crystals in the stools; sweating; excessive appetite; somewhat excessive thirst; and occasional anorexia.

Howland pointed out that the disease occurs at all ages of childhood. He noticed loose stools from time to time accompanied by loss of weight. According to Howland, the condition improves somewhat between attacks, but sooner or later a relapse occurs, and there is a renewed loss of weight. The relapses are increasingly severe. Eventually, there is a condition of marked malnutrition in a peevish, fretful, but often precocious child. The abdomen is distended, at first intermittently, then nearly constantly. The stools are never normal. Even between the attacks of diarrhea, they are large, light gray in color, often frothy, and usually very foul. Sometimes constipation alternates with diarrhea. Gas is passed in large amounts, and to this the distention is due. Howland continues that matters go on thus nearly indefinitely. All kinds of foods are tried, and many physicians are consulted. Growth suffers in proportion to the length of time that the symptoms persist, and many children are greatly below the average in height. Such chil-

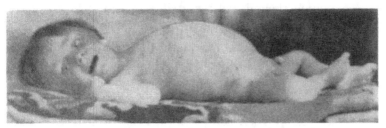

M. R., age 23 months.

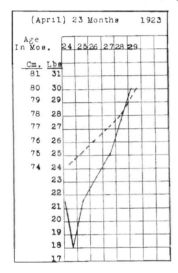

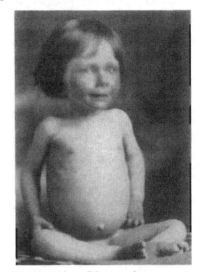

Age 24 months.

Progress of M. R. Length indicated by broken line, weight by straight line.

M. R., a boy, age 23 months, was presented for treatment April 27, 1923. His birth weight was 7 pounds (3.2 kg.). He was the second child. The first infant was normal. This patient was breast fed for two months, then breast and bottle fed, and after that had innumerable changes in diet. There was history of frequent attacks of diarrhea, occasional vomiting, excessive irritability and peevishness. He had otitis at the age of about 1 year, croup at the age of 18 months, and was said to have had an attack of intestinal grippe at the age of 1 year. He had never walked. Roentgen-ray examination of the legs is said to have shown scurvy and rickets. When he came under observation he was receiving the following diet: 6 A. M., milk, 5 ounces (148 cc.); 8 A. M., orange juice; 10 A. M., farina and milk; 12 NOON, soup, meat, vegetables and stewed fruit; 6 P. M., cereal, junket or custard and milk. The total amount of milk daily was 24 ounces (710 cc.). Total calories 900, or about 53 per pound.

Examination showed a desperately sick baby who looked as though he could not possibly survive. Very marked edema from the hips down. This was somewhat less marked in the upper extremities. The abdomen was markedly distended, 48½ cm. in circumference, and contained free fluid. The pallor was extreme. The child whimpered, was peevish and cried when touched. He did not move the lower extremities, and had a tendency to keep the hands over the eyes. The urine contained albumin with several hundred granular and granulohyalin casts to the field. The blood showed a distinct secondary anemia, 3,400,000 erythrocytes. The hemoglobin was 40 per cent. There was no abnormal cytology. Within four weeks the urine became normal. May 11, the patient was less irritable, smiled for the first time in weeks, the stools were improved, and the edema was much less. May 26, four weeks after coming under observation, there were from four to five stools daily, large, yellow and occasionally green. The child's appetite was ravenous. He was happy and smiled constantly. He received eight bananas, pot cheese made from one quart of milk, 24 ounces (710 cc.) of milk converted into protein milk by means of calcium caseinate, broth, the juice of an orange, and the white of one egg. June 27, 1923, he was taking from 14 to 16 bananas daily. August 6, 1923, the stools were normal except for an occasional slight amount of mucus. The child was no longer ravenous, and he was able to stand. The perspiration was profuse, with the odor of lactic acid. He was so fat that he looked edematous; he gained almost 3 pounds in eighteen days. October 13, the hemoglobin was 60 per cent and the erythrocytes 5,000,000. This child made very rapid progress, and on January 12, 1924, his height was 85 cm., his weight 32 pounds, 14 ounces (14.5 kg.). The stools were yellow and normal. He walked and was happy and well. Twenty years later he was found to be physically fit and became an officer in the U. S. Navy.

Age 22½ years

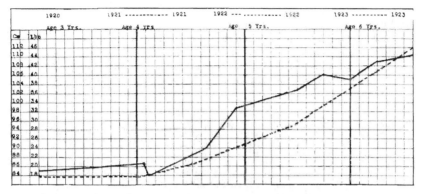

Progress of D. S. Broken line indicates height, straight line, weight.

D. S., a boy, age 4 years, was presented for treatment Oct. 10, 1921. His weight at that time was 20 pounds, 14 ounces (9 kg.). His height, 33 inches (84 cm.).

He had been brought to the office Oct. 7, 1920, presenting the same symptoms only to a less degree. At that time his weight was 19 pounds (8.6 kg.) and his height 33 inches (84 cm.). During the year there had been practically no gain in weight, the discrepancy being due to the increased edema, and no gain in the height. The family history was negative; the patient was the first of two children, born at full term, and a forceps delivery. There was bleeding from the umbilicus and generalized subcutaneous hemorrhages, lasting several days. There were no bleeders in the family. The patient had scurvy (?) when 7 months old for the duration of two weeks and again at the age of 2 years, while on a general diet, which however contained no vegetables, and again when 2 years and 3 months old. The hands, feet and face swelled up, and there was a history of vomiting, anorexia and thin stools during attacks. When the patient was brought the second time, he was receiving the following daily diet: At 6 A. M., 8 ounces of protein milk; at 10 A. M., farina, bread and butter, protein milk; at 2 P. M., strained vegetable soup, rice and carrots, hard-boiled egg, cottage cheese; at 6 P. M., cottage cheese, protein milk, bread and butter; and at 10 P. M., protein milk.

The physical examination at this time showed a child, who, although 4 years old, seemed to be an infant in arms, being carried in on a pillow. He had never sat, stood or walked. The most striking feature was the intense pallor and the unhappy facies, the patient whimpering constantly. When stripped, the abdomen showed great distention (circumference 63 cm.). His legs were flexed, the thighs abducted in a frog posture. They were practically without power. Handling seemed to cause him pain. The mouth was sore, and the child seemed to avoid light.

The edema was marked. There was considerable free fluid in the abdominal cavity. The following diet was ordered:

At 6 A. M., 9 ounces (266 cc.) of protein milk; at 8 A. M., orange and one banana; at 9 A. M., one banana, 7 ounces (207 cc.) of protein milk; at 12 NOON, scraped meat, two tablespoonfuls, and protein milk, 7 ounces; at 3 P. M., 9 ounces albumin

D. S., age 5½ years, to the left. Compare with a younger brother, age 4½ years

D. S., age 24 years

milk; at 6 P. M., whites of two eggs, gelatin, ½ ounce (15 cc.), and protein milk, 7 ounces; at 10 P. M., protein milk and banana.

This was soon increased, more bananas being given and pot cheese added. Sodium bicarbonate irrigations were used once or twice daily and a dose of castor oil given once a week. On this diet the edema, tenderness, anorexia and diarrhea disappeared. The child became happy, began to have a healthy color and progressed uninterruptedly, excepting for a short period of underfeeding when his weight fell off slightly, but with no symptoms of disease. At the present time he is a ruddy-looking child, playful, walks and runs, and is quite normal in every respect, except that he is underweight and undersized for his age, 5½ years, and that carbohydrates with the exception of banana must be very carefully restricted, and milk as such omitted entirely.

When seen on May 26, 1924, at the age of 6½ years, his weight was 45 pounds (20 kg.) and his height 43½ inches (111 cm.).

The photograph of the soldier in uniform was taken June, 1942. In the early thirties he had taken up soldiering as a career and was found to be entirely normal physically. At the present time, at the age of 34 and the father of a family, he is enjoying excellent health.

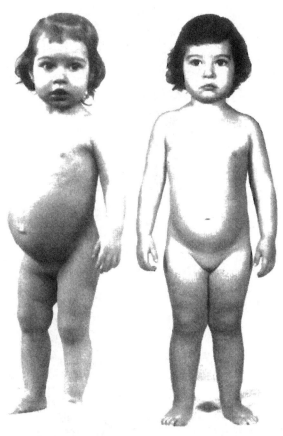

March 11, 1949
Age 16½ months
Height 29¾ in.
Weight 19 lbs. 14 oz.

December 7, 1949
Age 26 months
Height 33⅞ in.
Weight 29 lbs. 10 oz.

Gain in one year
Height 4 in.
Weight 10 lbs.

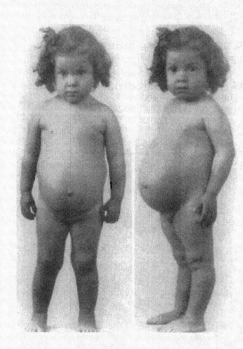

Tina A., January 11, 1949

Age 3 years, 2 weeks
Height 34 in.
Weight 35 lbs.
December, 1950

Age 5 years, 1 month
Height 41¾ in.
Weight 47¼ lbs.

First treated November 22, 1948
Edematous weight 32¼ lbs.
December 6 (2 weeks later) 27½ lbs.

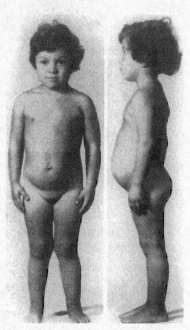

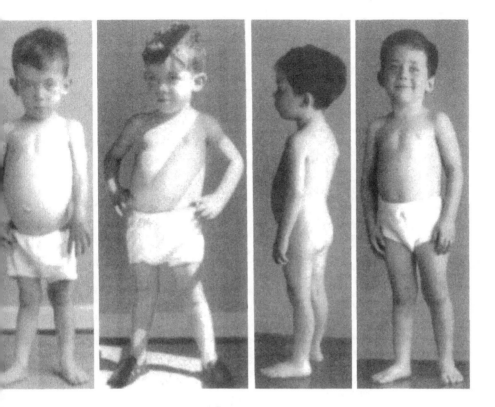

Howard B., age 3 years and 7 months. First seen July 9, 1950. There was a typical history of celiac disease (intermittent diarrhea, failure to grow or gain in weight during the previous 28 months). Numerous diets had been used, and he had been observed by very competent pediatricians.

He was put on a *carbohydrate specific* diet; the immediate effect upon his sense of well-being is most graphically shown in the following photographs (*left to right*):

	WEIGHT	HEIGHT
July 9, 1950	20¼ lbs.	33¾ in.
August 1, 1950 (3 weeks)	24¾ lbs.	
January, 1951 (6 months)	30 lbs.	36 in.
January, 1951		

As a result of this diet, after a cessation of growth for 28 months, his length increased at a rate 30 per cent and his weight at a rate 200 per cent above the average for his age.

dren are in danger from any intercurrent infection, especially one of the intestinal tract.

Although the diagnostic descriptions of Gee, Herter and Howland are by far the most valuable, it may be useful to mention other criteria that have been put forth by other investigators. Svensgaard [585] and Thaysen,[595] as well as others, have laid emphasis upon the significance of the low blood-sugar curve in diagnosing celiac disease. Harrison [247] and Sheldon,[549] as well as others, have emphasized the importance of a high fat content of the feces in diagnosing the condition. Schwachman, Farber and Maddock [541] have emphasized the importance of an assay of duodenal contents in differentiating between celiac disease and cystic fibrosis of the pancreas. They point out that while pancreatic achylia or hypochylia is a characteristic and constant finding in cystic fibrosis of the pancreas, there are relatively normal values for duodenal juices in celiac disease. Various other writers have also laid great stress on the importance of an assay of duodenal juices. According to Gerstenberger,[208] a simpler differential diagnosis between cystic fibrosis of the pancreas and celiac disease may be made by giving the patient carotene in oil. The diagnosis of pancreatic fibrosis can then be made simply by observing the diapers. All of the other symptoms described, such as various avitaminoses, anemia, large abdomen, hydrolability, emaciation, etc., are secondary rather than primary and are therefore of questionable diagnostic value.

15

Treatment

From the days of Gee to the present, the fundamental treatment for celiac disease has been dietary. At one time or another, various medications and supplements have been suggested and used, many of them of great help, but the basis of therapy has remained dietetic. The variety of diets recommended is startling, clear evidence that for much of the time celiac disease has been known, doctors have understood very little about it. The term, "celiac diet," has often been used as if it meant the same thing to all people, whereas there have been dozens of "celiac diets." Some writers have complained that patients did poorly on a "celiac diet" when no true celiac diet, based on an accurate understanding of the clinical features of the disease, was used at all. Many diets have, indeed, gone contrary to the most conclusive observations of the best investigators and seemingly have been based on little more than the whims of the doctor. Other diets have been constructed to fit theories about the disease and have been doggedly supported despite very high mortality among patients.

Some of the suggestions of Aretaeus [22] were almost as sensible as those promulgated 18 centuries later; certainly his inclusion of "the juice of the plantain" was interesting. Gee [205] saw the condition more clearly than many writers 30 years later. Although there was no sound reason for his exclusion of fruits and vegetables, many of his dietary suggestions were based upon excellent observation—notably that cow's milk could not be tolerated by the celiac patient. Many writers were suggesting some form of cow's milk 40 years later, despite the distress of their patients. Gee also observed that no highly starchy foods were fit for the celiac, but that meats, eggs and butter were satisfactory. Predigested foods were of no avail, he said, since peptonized milk and gruel were not tolerated. His most interesting observation was that with one patient a quart of the best Dutch mussels daily worked wonders. But with the end of the mussel season, the patient's trouble returned.

Cheadle,[104] basing some of his suggestions on his belief that the liver was defective in some way, used "hepatic stimulants." Like Gee, he saw that meats and fish were well borne, and he permitted fresh fruits. He recommended skimmed milk, doubtless on the theory that it was the fat in milk that caused the difficulty. Many writers even today cling to the same idea.

Schütz,[537] in 1904, took his diet almost as far as possible in the wrong direction by eliminating all fruits and vegetables. Heubner [258] kept to the right road more clearly when he recommended no fats or carbohydrates. But he also eliminated proteins in severe cases and then relied completely on mother's milk which contained the truly offending ingredients in substantial form. Herter's [253] observations were thorough and accurate. He found that proteins were very well borne, fats moderately well borne, and carbohydrates badly tolerated. But his concern with the role of bacteria prevented him from formulating a dietary regimen that, on the basis of his observations, might have been more successful than any suggested for many years to come. It is unfortunate, too, that no one seemed to notice Vipond's [627] work on diarrhea in children in 1911, in which banana flour and divi-divi brought such rewarding results.

As writers continued to stress the fatty stools and the apparent difficulty with fat metabolism, it was natural that diets emphasized the reduction or the elimination of fats from the diet, although prognosis under such diets was no more favorable than it had been before their introduction.

In 1920 Miller [389] suggested reduction but not elimination
of fats from the diet, but in 1923 he and Perkins [401] described
a diet which reduced fat to a minimum and replaced butter
with anchovy paste, potted meat, jams, sirups and honey.
Their use of chicken, eggs, lean meat and fish indicated that,
in common with most writers, they found proteins were well
borne. But their admission of bread and toast, plus the use
of skimmed milk, showed that the role of carbohydrates in
celiac disease had escaped them. Moorhead [416] suggested
rusks, jelly, raw beef juice and, despite Gee's finding 32 years
earlier, peptonized or plain milk.

Howland and Haas, working independently, suggested
diets based on the clinical observations of Herter concerning
carbohydrates. Howland [272] said that of all the elements of
food, "carbohydrate is the one which must be excluded
rigorously; that with this greatly reduced, the other elements
are almost always well digested, even though the absorption
of fat may not be as satisfactory as it is in health." His treatment, which was carried out in three stages, was a high-
protein diet based on protein milk, and it achieved greater
success than any previously set forth. But at the stage when
carbohydrates were added to the diet, he encountered frequent recurrence of symptoms.

In 1923 Haas [233] reported on the success achieved with a
similar high-protein diet to which he added banana and
other fruits and some vegetables. These supplied carbohydrates in a form that was well borne, even by advanced cases
of celiac disease. After this, a wider use of fruits and vegetables, especially the banana, may be noted in the literature,
although many investigators continued to view fats as the
chief offenders.

In 1922 Kleinschmidt [313] reported a diet based on protein
milk and mixed fats, carbohydrates, fruits and vegetables,
eliminating those foods which fermented readily. He found,
however, that he was unsuccessful in treating celiac disease

until he began to use the Haas diet, whereupon, in 1931,[314] he reported on the good results obtained.

Hablützel-Weber [238] recommended a high protein diet with drastic diminution of fats, carbohydrates, fruits and vegetables.

Fanconi [172] verified the efficacy of fruits and vegetables in the diet but used buttermilk or skimmed dried milk. He also observed that cane sugar and grain foods, even in small quantities, were decidedly unfavorable in their effects.

Courtin,[118] in 1933, reported that 8 of his cases died before he had tried the fruit-and-vegetable diet, but that after he instituted that therapy most of his patients not only lived but developed in a more or less normal fashion. He laid strong emphasis on his case histories as proving the value of the fruit-and-vegetable diet.

Marriott,[370] unaware of Haas' work, emphasized the important point that most celiac patients were not getting enough food. He eliminated fats and excluded those sugars which fermented readily. He saw the need of high protein intake, using buttermilk with milk protein added, beef and egg. For calories he used sugars, stating that they should be of the type not readily fermented. He recommended dextrines or brown corn sirup. He also used farina and baked potato, showing that he underestimated the importance of carbohydrates as a causative agent of celiac disease.

Kerley [309] found bananas a valuable adjunct to a high protein diet but replaced milk with a gruel containing some badly tolerated carbohydrates.

Lehndorff and Mautner [339] seemed to be discouraged about the benefit of any dietary therapy but mentioned the "banana diet" as approved by Irish,[283] Smith,[558] and Kerley and Craig.[310] In those days, however, the "banana diet" meant almost anything that included banana (an error that exists even today) and many such diets failed or produced poor results because they included other offending carbohydrates.

In an excellent paper, published in 1934, Schiff [583] reviewed the numerous diets suggested and named the two chief types in use as the high-protein diet and the Haas banana diet. He failed to see that the banana diet was also a high protein diet, but that carbohydrates were added in a form in which they were best tolerated. He laid stress on vitamin therapy and on psychotherapy. For several years and down to the present time all writers have recommended supplements of vitamins, especially A, D and B.

Many writers continued to recommend low fats in the diet, notably Parsons,[447] Snell et al.,[561] and Wall.[638] The last recommended protein or skimmed milk fortified with calcium caseinate. He also stated that apparently bananas were the only carbohydrates well tolerated and said that patients might eat from 4 to 6 a day. Hassmann,[248] in 1940, described an apple-and-banana diet. Two years later Gonce [220] outlined a diet which was high in protein, low in fat and low in carbohydrates, except those with invert sugars such as are contained in banana. He stressed that no cereals should be given.

In 1947 Andersen [16] outlined a diet high in protein and low in starch, abundant in vitamins. She was not emphatic about the reduction of fats, but reduced them rather sharply. And, despite the warnings against carbohydrates, she included rusks, lollipops and certain badly borne carbohydrates which always have been found to cause trouble, even when taken in minute quantities.

In 1946 Scott [545] reported a diet based on boiled skimmed milk. A year later Lewes [844] emphasized the efficacy of liver and vitamin B complex therapy. As for diet, he recommended skimmed milk, protein milk, or buttermilk, making no real distinction between them, although experience has shown that only protein milk is tolerated well. Next, he added carbohydrates in the form of dextrines and maltose and finally he added fat. He commented unfavorably on the emphasis placed on bananas in the diet by so many pediatricians, quoting Morse's [418] statement that "there is no reason for believing that bananas have any specific action in the treatment of this condition. They simply afford a convenient method of giving carbohydrates." From this statement the implication was deduced that the proponents of the use of banana claimed that this fruit had a medicinal therapeutic effect—a claim that never has been made. Bananas are used in a diet that has many other important features, simply because they afford a cheap, convenient and palatable source of well-tolerated carbohydrates. It is interesting to note that today, no one, regardless of the etiological or therapeutic viewpoint held, in practice treats celiac disease without including banana in the diet.

Other writers have made various dietary recommendations, Neale [426] adds intensive ultraviolet irradiations and liberal doses of vitamin D to a high protein, moderate carbohydrate, very low fat diet. Mitchell and Nelson's [405] textbook approves of Howland's three-phase diet with the addition of vitamins, liver extract and iron. Holt and McIntosh [267] point out that fats are avoided, that glucose and levulose seem to be better tolerated than polysaccharides and that protein is well digested. Brenneman [70] recommends a diet which is based on proteins, banana, vegetables, pot cheese, scraped apple and other fresh fruit, and lean meat. Carbohydrates and whole milk are added to this diet much earlier than in the diet which we recommend. May and his associates [374] recommended the parenteral administration of crude liver extracts and the vitamin B complex, maintaining that this therapy favorably influenced the absorption of fat in celiac disease as well as the intestinal motility, absorption of glucose, and the clinical course.

16

Prognosis

A survey of the literature from the point of view of prognosis yields very interesting results. It seems rather clear that the favorability of prognosis varies directly with the proximity of the diet to the carbohydrate specific diet which we shall detail in the last chapter of this work.

Gee [205] said that the course of the disease is always slow, whatever its end; whether the patient live or die, he lingers ill for months or years. Death is common and is mostly brought about by some intercurrent disorder. Recovery is complete or incomplete. When recovery tends to be complete, weakness of the legs is left long after all other tokens of the disease have passed away. When recovery is incomplete, the illness drags on for years, the patient getting better on the whole, but being very subject to relapses. While the disease is active, the children cease to grow. Even when it tends slowly to recovery, they are left frail and stunted. Gee's pessimistic prognosis continues throughout the literature even to this day.

Herter [258] points out that neglect means deterioration into a state of extreme involution, ending either in death or in a relatively fixed state of underdevelopment little ameliorated by any course of treatment at present known. Intelligent and careful treatment, on the other hand, leads to at least some degree of improvement and perhaps to a very striking betterment in nutrition and growth.

Heubner [248] says that the disease may continue for years with periods of improvement alternating with periods of deterioration. Growth and height are retarded for months or even years and in a large number of cases remain below normal for life, even if the disease is cured. A fatal outcome is not infrequent.

Freeman [195] is likewise pessimistic in his prognosis. He points out specifically that one of his cases did not appear to do well on carbohydrates.

Of the 41 cases on which Still [575] reported in his Lumelian lectures, 6 died, 27 were not cured, 5 returned to normal stools and nutrition but were permanently stunted, and only 3 were permanently improved.

The first really optimistic note was sounded by Howland [272] who noted that on his diet the patients did well. Many became vigorous and strong, some were left with no trace of dietary idiosyncrasies, while others were left with digestions that had to be treated with care. None, however, remained semi-invalids.

Hablützel-Weber [238] reported that 50 per cent of his cases made a complete recovery, while almost 40 per cent showed a substantial improvement. However, many cases remained undersize and underweight.

In 1924 S. V. Haas [233] reported that in cases in which the diet can be controlled for a sufficient length of time, recovery ensues in every instance and without nutritional relapse. This was the first report of the banana diet and the first really favorable prognosis.

In 1927 Lehndorff and Mautner [339] reported on a compilation of 218 cases with 34 deaths, a mortality of 15.6 per cent. They said that they knew of no medicine or dietary regimen that could be said to work definitely, and they expressed their belief that cases of marked celiac disease are of unfavorable prognosis.

Sauer,[522] on the other hand, in the same year, reported that the celiac syndrome disappears when fresh cow's milk, carbohydrates and fats are eliminated from the diet. He pointed out that prognosis depends on the diet rather than on the severity or the duration of the disease.

In 1928 Von den Steinen [632] reported on a study made at Ibrahim's clinic which substantiated the efficacy of Haas' diet and verified the favorable prognosis which results from it.

Kleinschmidt [313] also reported on the efficacy of the Haas diet, stating that "the prognosis in celiac disease has undergone a complete change during the last few years. The discouraging results of the previous methods of treatment have entirely disappeared since we have followed the diet of the American, Haas."

Parsons,[447] on the other hand, was still somewhat pessimistic concerning prognosis as late as 1932. In a paper published that year, he said: "Celiac disease runs a long drawn out course marked by many ups and downs. In spite of careful treatment, progress toward recovery is slow and intermittent, and diarrhea occurs from time to time, possibly from irregularities and premature changes in diet or from parenteral infections." He points out that catastrophes or crises occur, that the celiac child is often stunted permanently, and that the treatment is tedious and full of anxiety. Finally, he reports a mortality of 10.6 per cent.

Bargebuhr,[32] on the contrary, reported that the prognosis was good if a diet based on large quantities of bananas was given for at least a period of one year. He continued that with such a diet, there were no catastrophes and that the favorable prognosis was not altered whether the onset of the disease was mild or severe, or whether the disease started early in life or in later childhood.

Neale,[426] utilizing a fat-free diet, reported that the time required for complete recovery varied greatly, the shortest being two years. However, the time required for recovery in most cases was much longer.

In 1933 Courtin [118] reported on 34 cases. Significantly, he pointed out that the fatalities in his series took place before he used the fruit-and-vegetable diet. He stated that with the fruit-and-vegetable diet the prognosis for the disease is excellent, both from the point of view of mortality and of the ultimate attainment of perfectly normal development.

Holt and McIntosh [267] maintain that with intelligent treatment recovery occurs eventually in the large majority of cases, although stunting of growth is likely to persist. Brennemann's Practice [11] also points out that the course of recovery is a long one—two or more years—and, that although the ultimate prognosis for survival is uniformly good, there are some cases in which development is permanently retarded.

In 1939 Hardwick [243] reported on 73 cases of celiac disease which had been treated with various diets but not with the Haas diet. He reported a mortality of 30 per cent. Only 37 per cent of the cases appeared to have recovered completely, while the rest were still not fully recovered. Hardwick further pointed out that patients who have had celiac disease tend to remain dwarfed.

In 1938 Haas [235] published another paper, this time citing 134 consecutive cases of celiac disease. Of these, 3 died of disease completely unrelated to celiac disease. All of the rest recovered completely and were alive and well, some of them 15 years after their initial presentation.

In the same year Fanconi [174] also reported very favorable prognosis under treatment with his fruit-and-vegetable diet.

In 1950 S. V. and M. P. Haas,[237] reporting on 603 cases, all of them treated with the carbohydrate specific diet, pointed out that practically all cases recover completely and that there should be no deaths.

In recent years, some of the most prominent investigators have continued to issue most pessimistic reports on the ultimate prognosis of celiac disease. At a meeting of the American Academy of Pediatrics in 1950, one speaker pointed to a mortality of 5.17 per cent in a series of 58 cases. Furthermore, it was reported that only 10 cases were considered completely recovered; 23 patients, after the acute phase of the disease had passed, showed persistence of clinical and especially laboratory abnormalities. Most of the patients reported on at this meeting had a moderate or normal intake of starchy foods in their diet. The report concluded that the ultimate outlook made complete recovery from celiac disease improbable in the majority of cases.

17

Celiac Disease Today

A Concept Based on the Authors' Experience

This section will deal with the various aspects of celiac disease as we know it from clinical experience. We shall attempt to correlate our findings with many of the seemingly contradictory viewpoints and facts with which the literature on the subject is replete.

DEFINITION

First, one must delineate the frame of reference of the subject by attempting a definition of a disease picture which presents many aspects, depending upon the moment in a dynamic process which is selected for observation. For purposes of discussion, we define celiac disease as a condition, seen primarily in infancy and childhood, where there exists a prolonged intermittent diarrheal state resulting in various degrees of malnutrition. This condition occurs in the absence of specific organic disease and it may be reversed and caused to disappear by a specific mode of treatment. Further to enlarge on this definition: "prolonged" may mean a period of time ranging from a few weeks to many years; "intermittent" may refer to episodic occurrences for periods of days, weeks, or months; and "diarrheal" may be interpreted as increased frequency of stools from two or more with a change of normal consistency to soft, loose, or watery. "Specific organic disease" refers to such known etiologic agents of enteric disturbances as bacterial infections, extensive parasitic infestations, or structural abnormalities. It will be noted that we do not admit into our definition such vague etiologic concepts as "constitutional" or "metabolic" deficiencies, inasmuch as we feel that a definition, in order to be of value, should deal only with factors that are definitely recognized, even though such recognition be based on purely empirical evidence. This is not to imply that we shall not deal below with what appear to us as possible concepts of etiology.

DIAGNOSIS

From such a definition, then, the mode of diagnosis follows. It may be stated categorically that the diagnosis of celiac disease depends upon three factors: (1) history; (2) sufficient clinical and pathologic investigation to rule out the presence of other diseases of specific etiology; (3) response to appropriate therapy. We propose to discuss these diagnostic criteria in order.

Whenever an infant or a young child presents a history of two or more episodes of diarrhea, the possibility of celiac disease must be considered. The history may vary from cases where the occurrence of few to many soft, loose, or watery stools for a period of days or weeks is reported to cases in which the report indicates the occurrence of multiple intermittent episodes of loose frequent stools, alternating with periods of normal stools or even constipation and finally culminating in a period of months or even years where, although there may be only one or two stools a day, each of these is large, pale, greasy and of foul odor. The history will also show that if the periods of diarrhea have existed for a sufficiently long time, there is evidence of loss of weight, or at least failure to gain weight, and of failure to grow. The degree of retardation is, of course, dependent upon the duration and the severity of the disease. Another important feature in the history is the change in the psychological picture of the patient from a normal child to a depressed youngster who has developed severe behavior problems. Sometimes this change is reported to have taken place soon after the onset of the diarrheal episodes. By way of illustration, let us give examples of case histories of both extremes of celiac disease—mild cases and severe cases. These illustrations are synthesized from many actual histories which we have collected, and represent a cross-sectional view.

The mild case might be a two-and-a-half-year-old child, boy or girl, who is brought to the physician because he is having five loose, foul, mucus-laden stools a day. The parent may report that the child was colicky from birth and had frequent episodes of spitting and crying. The history may reveal that there was some difficulty with formulae during the first few weeks, not only because of the colic but also because of loose stools. However, changes of formula corrected the condition, and the child seemed to be normal until he reached the age of 6 months, when he suffered from diarrhea for 3 successive days. After this episode was cleared up, there was no further trouble until he was 9 months old, when there was another short period of diarrhea, which was controlled by boiling the child's milk. From the age of 9 months until the age of 2 years, there were perhaps 3 or more similar diarrheal episodes of short duration. At the age of 2, following a cold, the child suffered from diarrhea for a week, following which he continued to have 2 or 3 loose or soft stools each day. Various changes in diet were tried, and it was found that when the foods were severely limited in variety, the stools became normal. However when, after a few weeks on restricted diet, more foods were added, the diarrhea recurred, to be controlled only by a return to a regimen of severely restricted foods. Finally, a month before presentation, the child had had another cold which was followed by a few days of frequent watery stools. Since then there have been 4 or 5 loose stools a day, the child's appetite has become poor, he complains of abdominal pains, and he is irritable, cries, whines, has temper tantrums and seems to be listless. He still appears to be well nourished, but during the past month he has lost a little weight.

At the other extreme, is the three-or-four-year-old whose early history is similar to that of the mild case. At the age of 2, however, the stools became less frequent—perhaps only one a day—but took on the appearance of a huge, gray, glistening, foul, porridgelike mass. From this time on, although there might be days when there was no movement at all, most movements that did occur were abnormal. Along with the large bulky stools, there developed rapid loss in weight, general weakness and marked irritability. The appetite, usually anoretic but occasionally bulimic, has become capricious. During this period, the body contour has changed markedly. There has been loss of subcutaneous fat, so that the buttocks are flat, and the limbs spidery. The child has developed an enormous potbelly, and his facial aspect is pinched and unhappy. These, then, may be considered as paradigms of the two extremes. In the first instance—the mild—the physician may be hard pressed to determine "how many swallows make a summer." In the second—a full-blown and classical case of severe celiac disease—the diagnosis is clear.

So far as clinical pathology is concerned, the picture in the severe case of long duration is clear. The patient will show evidence of wasting and absence of subcutaneous fat as exemplified by flat buttocks and spidery limbs. He will have a huge potbelly. He will show evidences of various and/or multiple avitaminoses, such as scurvy, weakness, edema, and signs of vitamin B deficiencies. In the mild case, however, the physical examination may show the child to be in an excellent nutritional state.

In both extremes the patient may show psychological symptoms of significance. In a questionable mild case, when a child displays marked irritability, capriciousness, or tantrums, the probability of celiac disease is strengthened.

Hematologic examination will be helpful only in ruling out the possibility of blood diseases or parasitic infestations of the blood stream. The presence or the absence of anemia will depend on the severity and the duration of the malnutrition which is a concomitant of celiac disease.

Examination of the stool will be of assistance primarily in eliminating the possibility of a severe parasitic infestation or bacterial infection of the intestinal tract. Much has been written about fat in the stool, but examination for this purpose is useful only if the fat content of the feces is found to be markedly elevated. By definition, a marked elevation of stool fat indicates a steatorrhea. While celiac disease is the principal cause of this condition, steatorrhea occurs in other diseases as well. The "eel under the rock," so far as examination of the stool for fat is concerned, is that in celiac disease the occurrence of steatorrhea is a variable which depends on the severity of the diarrhea at the moment when the specimen for examination is passed. If, in a mild case, the disease is not in a phase which results in brisk diarrhea, the stool fat may not be elevated, so that a finding of normal fat content of the stool in no way excludes the diagnosis of celiac disease.

At one time it was postulated that the finding of starch granules in the stool bespoke the presence of a disease entity called "starch intolerance"—a condition distinct from celiac disease. Although this concept has since been retracted by its originator, the description of this so-called entity is still found in standard texts, and some practitioners continue to treat celiac disease according to this concept. The discovery of starch granules in the stool is of dubious significance because their presence depends upon the briskness of the diarrhea at the time of the collection of the sample. If there are frequent loose movements, the intestinal passage time is short, and many items of ingested material may be found in the stool. Moreover, the feeding of banana to a normal child will result in the appearance of many extracellular (outside of the banana fiber) starch granules in the stool. In celiac cases who receive no other form of starch but that contained in the banana, the stools will all show such starch granules and will show them in an amount proportional to the amount of banana which is ingested. Therefore, the presence of starch granules in the stool serves to obfuscate rather than to illuminate the diagnosis of celiac disease.

Work done in the past few years has stressed that the lysis of a gelatin film by a stool indicates the presence of trypsin, and that this test can be used to distinguish cystic fibrosis of the pancreas from celiac disease. In the first place, it should be emphasized that the action on which this test is based cannot be solely attributed to pancreatic trypsin because the stool contains many protolytic factors, both from the child himself and from the organisms which inhabit his intestinal tract. However, if later work continues to show that stools from most cystic fibrosis cases do not cause lysis of a gelatin film, this test may be useful as a screening device to distinguish cystic fibrosis from celiac disease.

The study of duodenal enzymes is fraught with technical difficulties and resultant errors. The outstanding problems are the difficulty of intubation of the duodenum even under fluoroscopic control, the dilution of the pancreatic juice by gastric juices as well as by bile and other juices, and the dilution error factors inherent in the methods of enzyme assay once a sample has been obtained. The most that can be said for this test is that an appreciable trypsin content rules out the possibility of cystic fibrosis of the pancreas. However, it is difficult to place much faith in a method where the normal figures for trypsin content of the duodenal juices carry a standard deviation equal to the mean.

An analysis of blood sugar is useful in excluding the possibility of diabetes. It was once thought that a flat glucose tolerance curve was a characteristic of celiac disease. However, it is now recognized by most investigators that the flat curves reported were merely expressions of the poor states of absorption which were characteristic of the disease during periods of severe diarrhea. However, why it was ever necessary to go to such lengths to demonstrate this fact when the practised clinician's eye or the office scales could more readily show it still remains a mystery.

Intestinal x-ray examination by barium is useful in ruling out the presence of congenital or postnatal anomalies, such as intestinal shunts or obstructive lesions of various sorts. As to the question of the value of the moulage or segmentation pattern, it has now been shown that this is characteristic of many vitamin deficiency states and not delineative of celiac disease. However, if the segmentation pattern exists, it may add somewhat to the diagnosis. The question as to the type of intestinal activity found in celiac disease has been raised in the literature. Some authors, although presenting insufficient evidence, reported hypomotility, while others maintained that they found hypermotility. From the clinical characteristics of the disease, especially the frequent passage of loose stools, deductive reasoning tends to corroborate those who report hypermotility of the gut. It is quite probable that both observations are entirely correct and that the seeming contradiction can be resolved in terms of the status of the case at the time of examination. If the patient was in a brisk diarrheal stage, hypermotility would have been observed; in a quiescent phase, however, hypomotility would have been evidenced as a "rebound" phenomenon. A chest roentgenogram is useful in ruling out the possibility of tuberculosis and in helping to differentiate between celiac disease and cystic fibrosis. Roentgenograms of the bones may reveal such abnormalities as rickets, scurvy, osteoporosis, etc. The degree of such abnormalities will depend on the patient's state of malnutrition but will not cast any significant light on the diagnosis of celiac disease per se.

Bacteriologic and serologic studies, especially of stool cultures, are most useful in excluding the presence of specific enteric infection. Other procedures may help to rule out other specific infections, such as tuberculosis, syphilis, etc. One aspect of bacteriology that should be mentioned is the early report of finding a specific organism, *Bacillus bifidis,* in the stools of sufferers from celiac disease. Although this finding has received little attention in recent years, it should be borne in mind as a possible avenue of research.

Given a case where the history indicates celiac disease and where the clinical pathology excludes other disease entities, the diagnosis of celiac disease can be fully proved by the following test and by the manner in which the patient responds to appropriate treatment. The following procedure should be followed. The child should be given a diet which excludes all carbohydrates, except those present in fruits and vegetables, and includes a large protein portion as well as an adequate fat portion. (The details of this proper celiac diet or better-named carbohydrate specific diet are detailed later.) In a period of time ranging from about 1 to 12 weeks, the diarrhea will clear. Then the child should be given liberal quantities of bread, sugar, potatoes and other carbohydrates in addition to the prior diet. If the child develops diarrhea again the diagnosis of celiac disease is absolute, and proper dietary therapy for a sufficient length of time must be employed.

In summary, the diagnosis of celiac disease is made on the basis of three considerations: (1) a history of prolonged intermittent diarrhea with a nutritional state dependent upon the duration and the severity of the disease; (2) the exclusion of other disease entities by means of clinical pathology; (3) correction of the diarrhea by carbohydrate specific diet and recurrence of diarrhea by the inclusion of carbohydrates other than those found in fruits and vegetables. The third point need be applied only in cases where any doubt remains after the application of the first two.

While the problem of differential diagnosis has been touched upon, it might be well to discuss more fully a few of the similar disease states and even the postulated diseases that must be borne in mind and ruled out in making a diagnosis of celiac disease.

Specific bacterial infections, overt parasitic infestations and anatomic anomalies should present very little difficulty in differentiation. However, we shall discuss in more detail a few possibilities that deserve more extended treatment.

The first of these is cystic fibrosis of the pancreas, a condition occurring in early infancy and childhood. This disease presents a clinical picture which may be identical with that of celiac disease—intermittent prolonged diarrhea, malnutrition and potbelly. In addition, however, this condition is almost always associated with repeated and persistent upper respiratory infections which ultimately result in chronic cough and pulmonary fibrosis. There are two factors which, *sui generis*, set cystic fibrosis aside from celiac disease: (1) chronic respiratory infection, purulent bronchiolitis, culminating in pulmonary fibrosis; (2) postmortem findings of a fibrotic and cystic pancreas. The point which leads many to differentiate this as a separate disease entity is that the same pathologic picture which is seen in the pancreas in a case of cystic fibrosis has also been found in the early neonatal period of infants succumbing to meconium ileus and in children who have died in the first few months of life from severe pulmonary infection usually diagnosed as bronchopneumonia. In neither of these conditions does the question of stool abnormality play anything but an equivocal role. The distinguishing pathologic feature of cystic fibrosis, aside from the upper respiratory infection and the x-ray finding of pulmonary fibrosis, is a trypsin content of the duodenal juices that is so low that most authors report it as absent. Whether cystic fibrosis of the pancreas is a distinct disease entity or whether it represents a group of celiac cases where the malnutrition is so severe that the child's resistance has been lowered to a point which has permitted the lungs and the pancreas to become fibrotic, we are not prepared to say now. However, regardless of what the final decision on this point may be, we have come to one very positive conclusion. That is, if cystic fibrosis of the pancreas is treated by the same dietary regimen that is used in celiac disease, the diarrhea will cease, nutrition will become normal, and if the pulmonary infiltration has not become too severe, it too will clear up. We have under treatment 4 such cases, 2 of which have been under observation for 6 years, and they are normal in all respects. One, who had far advanced pulmonary fibrosis, has excellent nutrition and normal stools but still suffers from a chronic cough. Another, who began treatment at the age of 6 weeks, now, at 6 months, has normal stools and nutrition and never has developed pulmonary signs.

The next conditions to be considered do not exist in actuality and are mentioned here only because the habit of textbook reprinting has perpetuated them in the literature, even though their originator has now retracted the idea of their existence. Historically, their names as disease entities arose when Dorothy Andersen, writing in the late thirties, attempted to subdivide celiac disease into a number of separate entities and postulated idiopathic steatorrhea, cystic fibrosis of the pancreas, starch intolerance and infantile steatorrhea as subdivisions. In the late forties, however, she retracted this idea. The disease of "starch intolerance" was described as a prolonged intermittent diarrhea in which bouts of diarrhea occurred in connection with upper respiratory infections, without steatorrhea or malnutrition, and with starch granules in the stools during diarrheal phases. Obviously, this is merely mild celiac disease where severity or duration have not been sufficient for steatorrhea to become evident. As we have mentioned earlier, starch granules are found in the stool if the passage time is fast enough or if sufficient quantities of banana are ingested, even with normal passage time. "Infantile steatorrhea" was described as intermittent diarrhea and steatorrhea occurring in the first year of life without abnormality of the duodenal enzyme activity. This subdivision was made necessary because celiac disease did not occur supposedly until the first or the second year, and because the normal duodenal enzyme activity ruled out the possibility of cystic fibrosis of the pancreas. These, it is obvious, represent cases of celiac disease which occur earlier than the usual age. It is interesting to note that even at the time that "infantile steatorrhea" was postulated, a reservation was provided by stating that it might represent celiac disease at an early age.

Two other disease states are sometimes mentioned in discussing celiac disease. Especially in the Latin American literature, much emphasis is given to parasitic infestations as a clinical state favoring the development of the celiac picture. Though it is true that a heavy infestation may give a picture of diarrhea and malnutrition, it is a mistake to label all such cases in which ova are found in the stools as parasitic infestations and to end the diagnosis at that point. It is much wiser to continue the patient under observation after the infestation has been eradicated and then, if the celiac symptoms continue, to consider a diagnosis of celiac disease. Something of the same point of view must be taken when the second disease state, allergy, is considered. While it is quite true that there are rare cases in which specific food allergies may set up a picture of chronic diarrhea, one must be very cautious in making a final diagnosis of allergy. In order to postulate allergic reaction as the cause of a persistent and intermittent diarrhea, two factors must be present: (1) a strong history of familial allergy and evidence of other forms of allergic reactions in the child; (2) the immediate connection between the ingestion of a specific food, such as egg or milk, and the occurrence of vomiting and diarrhea. Of course, it has been stated that the fact that any carbohydrates other than those found in fruits and vegetables or protein milk causes diarrhea and the other symptoms indicates that celiac disease is an allergic reaction to certain carbohydrates. However, this is stretching the concept of allergy beyond the breaking point, especially when one remembers that the occurrence of allergic manifestations and family history of allergy is no more frequent among celiac patients than among the general population.

SYMPTOMATOLOGY

Although we have already mentioned the symptoms of celiac disease, we feel that symptomatology should be discussed in greater detail. The invariable symptoms are prolonged intermittent diarrhea and psychogenic changes, including marked irritability and capriciousness. All other symptoms vary according to the duration and the severity of the disease. The evidences of malnutrition may vary from simple failure to gain weight to extreme emaciation with complete loss of subcutaneous fat, flat baggy buttocks, extreme interference of growth leading to stunted stature, weakness and easy fatiguability, atonic musculature with typical potbelly, secondary anemia of varying degrees, peripheral edema and intermittent abdominal cramps. The appetite may be capricious—good or even voracious at times but almost absent in most cases. There may be multiple vitamin deficiencies. The stools may be formed or loose and soft with a foul odor, or they may present the classical celiac stool picture—large, bulky, foul, pale and greasy. The number of movements may vary from none without assistance to as many as 10 or more a day, depending upon the severity of the disease, diet, or the presence of upper respiratory infection. The occurrence of "catastrophe" or "crisis," a state referred to in the literature but never encountered in our own experience, should be mentioned here. Such "crises" occur when there develops a sudden onset of brisk watery diarrhea which leads, in a short time, to dehydration, electrolyte loss, and shock requiring prompt and vigorous intravenous replacement therapy.

The distribution of celiac disease between the sexes is about equal.

The age distribution at the onset of the disease may vary from soon after birth to 3 or 4 years, with the majority of cases beginning in the 18-month to 30-month group. Although most cases are positively diagnosed at about the age of two, in a very large number, careful taking of the history will elicit a report of prior short episodes of bowel abnormality so that the exact age of onset is difficult to determine.

No definite statement concerning the incidence of celiac disease can be made here. Physicians who are interested in the disease may see many cases, while others may encounter very few. We might guess that while the average doctor may see only one or two cases a year, he may be able to recognize more if he is aware of the fact that the recurrence of abnormal bowel movements may indicate the possibility of celiac disease. It is interesting to note that very few cases are seen in the large free general pediatrics clinics in New York City.

The familial background of the patient is important, since it is not at all unusual to find the disease in siblings and cousins. As a matter of fact, we have treated four children of a physician, all of whom had celiac disease and another family with 5 cases. The economic level of the family seems to have little to do with the disease, nor do national or racial origins. With the exception of colic or vomiting in the neo-natal period, which appears in the histories of a significant proportion of cases, no other prior disease states seem to have any connection with celiac disease. Early diet seems to bear no relationship to the disease, nor does the time at which solid foods were introduced, nor does the question of breast or bottle feeding.

There is no marked or specific pathologic picture in celiac disease. The findings are those of marked malnutrition without noteworthy organ findings.

A consideration of physiology again reveals the dynamic character of celiac disease. In the mild or early case there may be no apparent abnormality other than the intestinal dysfunction. In such cases intestinal hypomotility may alternate with normal activity. In the severe and long-standing cases the physiologic changes will be those resulting from poor intestinal absorption of nutrients. These may include subnormal values for serum protein, calcium and phosphorus; microcytic hypochromic anemia; low vitamin A absorption curves; low fasting blood sugar and flat glucose tolerance curves; secondary osteoporosis, caused by the formation of calcium soaps by the excessive fatty acids in the gut; occasional rickets and xerophthalmia due to impaired fat-soluble vitamin absorption; an atonic small intestine, part of which has static loops, while other parts have contracted segments.

TREATMENT

The proper treatment of celiac disease can be stated very briefly—a proper diet for a sufficiently long time. One basic principle of the diet must be established firmly and reiterated persistently: *No food may be ingested by the celiac patient that contains an appreciable amount of carbohydrate other than that found in fruits and to a lesser extent in vegetables and in protein milk.* While this principle may be easily understood, it is difficult in practice always to recognize the existence of carbohydrates in various foods. Carbohydrates other than those designated often creep into the diet in small quantities unless the strictest attention is paid to every item of food.

The basis of the specific carbohydrate diet is ripe banana and protein milk. Protein milk should be prepared in one of the three ways described in the footnote below;* when the child will not drink protein milk, calcium caseinate milk* may be used.

---

* Protein milk prepared according to Finkelstein and Meyer: One quart milk, warmed to temperature of 98° Fahrenheit. To this is added one tablespoon of essence of pepsin. Allow to drain through cheesecloth for one half hour to separate the whey from the curd. The curd mixed with one pint of water is then rubbed through a fine wire strainer several times, and to it one pint of buttermilk is added. The whey, which contains most of the sugar, is discarded.

Although all fruits may be used later, banana is the most satisfactory and the only safe fruit to be used at the outset of the treatment. Its particular value in celiac disease comes from the fact that it is a 20 per cent carbohydrate and thus replaces better than any other fruit the excluded carbohydrates, such as cereal, bread, sugar and potatoes. It has a very low fiber content, is easily obtainable, palatable and well liked by most children. It may be served raw or baked. Only fully ripe bananas are desirable, with no trace of green at the tips, the skin well speckled with brown, and the edible portion soft enough to mash easily. In the unripe banana, most of the carbohydrate is in the form of starch which is converted, in the process of ripening, to sugars which the celiac patient tolerates well.

If ripe bananas are not available or impractical to use, banana powder may be substituted as the exact equivalent of fully ripe bananas.

Because various other fruits have qualities which tend to make them laxative, they must be employed judiciously when diarrhea is still active. There need be no curtailment of the amount of banana given. Most canned fruits are forbidden because of the added sugar. If cooked fruits are desired, they may be prepared at home with saccharin, but the initial product must be known.

The specific carbohydrate diet, in addition to protein milk

Protein milk as prepared by Mueller and Kran: Mix one quart of buttermilk (commercial) and one quart of water and heat to a temperature of 135° F. Remove from the stove and let stand for one half hour. By this time the curd is well separated from the whey, 36 oz. of which should be dipped off. The remaining curd and whey are mashed through a fine sieve, and 4 oz. of 20 per cent cream, or 4 oz. from top of bottle of milk, and enough water should be added to bring the mixture to 32 oz.

Powdered protein milk: 12 tablespoons of the powder to 32 oz. of water.

Calcium caseinate milk: Use from 4 to 6 tablespoons of calcium caseinate (Mead Johnson's Casec) to one pint of water and one pint of milk. Mix the Casec with a little cold water (enough to form a smooth paste), pour in the remainder of the cold water. Then pour in the milk and bring the whole mixture to a boil while stirring constantly and boil actively for one minute. Remove from fire. Let cool. If necessary to sweeten, use one or two tablets of saccharin (1 gr.).

"Hi-Pro" cannot be successfully used as a substitute for any of the above.

and fruits, may contain proteins in any form and fats in moderate quantities. Thus meat, fish and fowl of any kind may be used, and it is not necessary or even advisable to have all the fat removed. All cheese is satisfactory, unless it has been processed by the addition of ingredients to alter its composition; the diet may include any cheese in its initial form: Swiss, cheddar, American, and of course pot cheese.

Gelatine is given for dessert in this diet, but not Jello or other prepared gelatine desserts which contain sugar. Desserts made from pure gelatine, fruit juice, and saccharin for sweetening are well tolerated. Honey, dates and raisins may be used as confections, since they are chiefly monosaccharides, but some dates are packed in sugar sirup to make them adhere in one mass, and these should not be used.

When the brisk diarrhea is controlled, egg is added to the diet. When the stools are formed and occur no more than two or three times daily, vegetables are given. But they must be added to the diet cautiously, one at a time with a sufficient period between each new introduction to determine their effect. In some instances diarrhea recurs when vegetables are ingested, in which case their use must be postponed. In general, lettuce, squash, tomato, string beans and carrots are well tolerated. Canned vegetables are not used because many have sugar added. Potatoes are not used.

Fats in association with meats in the normal amount, in butter and in the protein milk are well borne. Sour cream is usually tolerated. The only restriction on fats may come at the beginning of the diet, but when a full and well-rounded diet has been established, there need be no restrictions of fat beyond those usually exercised in the diets of healthy children.

With the inclusion of the foods mentioned, the specific carbohydrate diet is complete. Since it is full and well balanced, it is continued for at least one year, supplemented by certain vitamins. Vitamins A and D should be administered, but cod-liver oil is usually not well tolerated. Some of the newer preparations of aqueous soluble A and D are excellent substitutes. One of the preparations of B complex, including folic acid, seems to be desirable. Since anemia is a regular feature of celiac disease, iron in some form is called for.

In prescribing this diet it is almost more important to stress what is *not* fed than what is fed. Any cereal grain is strictly and absolutely forbidden, including corn, wheat, rye, or rice in any form, whether as bread, cake, toast, zweiback, crackers, cookies, or breakfast cereals. Potato is prohibited. Sugar is forbidden as sweetening or in the form of candy, pastries, breads, etc., as well as dextrins such as are found in corn sirups and lollipops. Milk other than protein milk is not allowed.

The strictness of this diet cannot be overemphasized, nor should the difficulty of adhering to it be minimized. Faithful observance requires intelligence and vigilance on the part of the mother or the person taking care of the child with celiac disease. It is surprising how many times a child will, despite the best parental supervision, manage to get hold of forbidden food. It is equally surprising how many parents of apparent intelligence will, despite all warnings, decide that "just a taste" of ice cream, cookie, or candy will do no harm. Nevertheless, treatment is best carried out in the home, with frequent visits to the doctor's office. Of the cases reported here, only two were hospitalized.

At the beginning of the treatment the patient is put on a so-called basic diet:

Breakfast: Pot cheese, bananas, protein milk

Lunch: Meat, pot cheese, bananas, protein milk

Supper: The same as lunch; gelatine may be added to any meal

Any of these foods may be used in any quantity or given between meals.

After one week, orange juice, other cheeses and egg may be added, one at a time and with a sufficient interval to test the acceptability of each. After two weeks, all fresh fruits may be tried in the same way. When stools are controlled, vegetables (except potato and corn) may be added; sometimes they are well tolerated but often their introduction must be postponed. Tolerance is eventually attained, at which time the diet is complete.

If, at the beginning of the treatment, there is clinical evidence of gastro-intestinal hyperactivity such as colic or vomiting, as is frequently the case, this may be controlled by suitable doses of atropine.

Most cases begin to improve immediately. The earliest sign of improvement is a change in the child's disposition; he becomes happy, smiling, contented. The diarrhea is often controlled in the first week, but in some cases, such control may take a month or several months more. If he suffered from anorexia, the child's appetite improves, and he begins to grow and gain weight. During the first period of 6 months or more, any infection, especially in the upper respiratory tract, may be accompanied by a recurrence of the diarrhea. Also in this period the ingestion of a forbidden carbohydrate will bring about loose stools within hours or days, but the attack will quickly subside if no more of the forbidden food is ingested. A break in the diet after about 6 months will not usually be reflected immediately in diarrhea, but the ingestion of forbidden carbohydrates must be continued for some time, even weeks, for the diarrhea to recur. Otherwise, there are no relapses or so-called crises or catastrophes such as those described in much of the literature on the subject and requiring therapy to combat acidosis and dehydration.

Duration of the treatment is of utmost importance. The strict celiac diet must be continued for at least one year. If there has been no recurrence of symptoms, forbidden carbohydrates may be added; one slice of bread three times daily, or a bowl of cereal once and bread twice; or cereal at break-

fast, toast at lunch, and spaghetti for supper. If these additions to the diet cause no diarrhea, then potato is given.
After 3 months with no disturbance, plain milk is added, and
if no diarrhea occurs in the next 3 months with these additional foods, the patient may be considered cured, and all
restrictions on the diet may be lifted. As a rule, the entire
cure requires no more than 18 months, but when the diet
has not been followed rigorously, it may take a much longer
time.

When cure is obtained, there should be no relapse. A
striking example of the persistence of the disease in a case
where the proper diet was not followed is given by one of
our patients who was treated up to the age of 6 years. We
were unable to get the child to follow the proper regimen
because her mother owned a candy store and it was impossible
to keep the patient from forbidden carbohydrates. At the
age of 22 she returned to us with all the symptoms that she
had had in childhood, which had continued throughout the
years. Placed on a strict celiac diet which she followed faith-
fully, soon all symptoms disappeared. She is now, 2 years
later, apparently cured, and has been on a completely unrestricted diet without return of symptoms for 6 months.

Among milder cases of celiac disease, there is a degree of
tolerance for carbohydrates which allows for careless treatment with fair results, but cure requires two or three times as
long as would be the case if a strict celiac diet were followed.
In some such cases, the symptoms are little relieved, but
physical progress is maintained so as to obscure the fact that
a cure has not been obtained. Fortunately, time eventually
seems to help these cases to get well, although many of them
go through life with a tendency toward loose stools.

This diet differs, in varying degrees, from all those previously advocated in the literature on the subject. The basic
difference is that our diet excludes *all* carbohydrates except
those in fruits, some vegetables, and in protein milk. Many
other diets prescribe low carbohydrates but fail to specify

the type of carbohydrate. This designation of the proper type of carbohydrate to be fed is of the utmost importance, as experience in the above cases shows that even the smallest quantity of the forbidden carbohydrates will precipitate diarrhea.

Since the common factor to be found in all fruits appeared to be levulose and glucose, we were led to try any food in which these occurred. Thus honey and dates were used and found to be fully tolerated.

To test the hypothesis that levulose was a satisfactory form of sugar in celiac disease, we obtained a supply of pure levulose through the Sugar Research Foundation from the University of Colorado. We took a group of children suffering from celiac disease whose diarrhea and other symptoms were controlled and whose progress was satisfactory. They showed recent histories of diarrhea for a day or two following the accidental eating of a lollipop, bread, cookie, or other forbidden carbohydrate. To these children we gave levulose daily in liberal quantities. In every case we found that it could be taken without ill result.

Many diets put forward in standard works on celiac disease restrict the use of fat, ascribing the cause of the disease to both fat and carbohydrate intolerance or to fat intolerance alone. The evidence behind such beliefs is the frequent occurrence of steatorrhea in the disease. But it has been shown that fat is found in the stool even in a fat-free diet; and our experience in the 370 cases treated is that fat does not provoke diarrhea. All of our cases were fed fat in reasonable amounts during the course of treatment. When the whole dietary is low, fat must be somewhat restricted, as it would be in the feeding of normal children; when proteins and carbohydrates derived from fruits are increased in the diet, fat may be taken in the usual quantities. It should not be considered as a restricted food. Its absence from the diet is probably a contributory cause of lack of growth.

Many diets used in celiac disease call for the use of protein milk but fail to specify the type of protein milk. Many modified forms of protein milk have been devised, but our series of cases indicates that the only satisfactory product is protein milk prepared according to one of the three methods given in the footnote on page 128, or calcium caseinate milk. In all of these the sugar content is low. All others should be avoided.

Although the above dietary regimen is the basis of treatment, other modes of therapy have been considered and some of them tried. They should be mentioned briefly:

Vitamin B Complex and Liver Extract. From histories of our own cases and from the literature on the subject, it is found that injections of these substances will in many cases end diarrhea for a variable period of time. But diarrhea usually recurs when such injections are stopped. This treatment is painful and is disliked by patients.

Antibiotics and Sulfonamides. The use of antibiotics and sulfonamides is usually followed by cessation of diarrhea, but the diarrhea will recur after a period of discontinuance and sometimes even while the medication is being given.

Pancreatic Extract. It is not often used by us because dietary treatment gives the desired results. There is an occasional case in which the addition of pancreatic extract seems to be a useful adjuvant.

With the diet outlined, it would appear that the treatment would proceed simply. This, however, is a fallacy, because the niceties of clinical management present numerous difficulties. It is not sufficient to give the parents the proper diet and then to let the matter rest. It is necessary to educate the parents in the proper application of the regimen by constant checking and rechecking. If it were only the errors of ignorance that had to be overcome in the parents, the problem would not be too difficult. However, there **are** errors in treatment stemming from accident and from willful mismanagement. The accidental errors are those where a child is not sufficiently guarded and obtains candy, bread, or cookies from the family larder, from siblings, or even by stealing them from other children. Patient and persistent training of the parents can overcome this error. The real difficulty arises in willful mismanagement when the parents feel so sorry for the child that they give him "just a taste" of a forbidden carbohydrate. However, after a few disastrous experiences as a result of such "treats," most parents will develop control, although there is an occasional parent who is very slow to respond. This problem is comparable with that involved in maintaining a diabetic on his diet. Even when errors on the part of the parents have been overcome, there remains a source of difficulty in grandparents, friends, etc.

Once the dietary control has been achieved, most problems are solved. However, in the initial period of diet, say the first 3 to 6 months, the occurrence of upper respiratory or other infections is very prone to set off a period of loose and frequent stools lasting for a few days to a week. This is especially true during periods when the type of viral infection which causes mild intestinal symptoms in normal people is endemic. The important job of the physician during the diarrheic period brought on by infection is to be sure that the setback is, in reality, caused by such an infection and not by the ingestion of forbidden carbohydrates. He should also reassure the parents that the diarrhea is transitory and that it will not affect the final cure. It might be mentioned that during such infections the use of antibiotics, such as penicillin, or the sulfonamides will often cause immediate cessation of the diarrheal episode, even though there is evidence that the low-grade upper respiratory infection continues.

18

Course

The course of celiac disease, without proper treatment, is long, arduous and disappointing and marked by frequent setbacks which cause great anxiety to patient and parents alike. However, this is not true if proper treatment with a strict carbohydrate specific diet is instituted and carried out for a sufficient length of time. In our experience, when a carbohydrate specific diet is followed carefully, the first noticeable change in the child is not the cessation of diarrhea or the gain in weight, but the improvement in behavior. This has been so striking that we feel that it should be strongly emphasized as an important guide to therapy.

The usual course under proper treatment is that within a week or two after institution of the diet, the child is no longer irritable, petulant, or demanding. Instead of whining and crying and on the one hand clinging to its mother while it behaves aggressively to others, the child smiles, relaxes, plays calmly and does not act antisocially. The child who, but a week earlier, presented serious behavior problems, is now tractable and social. During the first few weeks the weight will either remain stationary or will even drop slightly. This drop is due to the loss of edema fluid, even though there be no overt clinical evidence of edema before the inception of the treatment. After this the psychological picture will continue to improve, and now gains in both weight and growth will be recorded. As to the course of the stools, we have had a few cases in which there was a cessation of the frequent and loose stools and a substitution of formed and completely normal stools within a few days after inception of the diet. However, the majority of cases will continue to have two or three soft (though not loose, watery, or foul) stools for a number of weeks, or months depending upon the duration of symptoms before initiating proper treatment. On the average, we should judge that the stools may be expected to become formed between the second and the sixth weeks, although we have seen a few cases where the stools did not become completely normal until the patient had followed the diet for two or three months.

Once the stools have become formed, they will remain so except for two causes. The most important of these is a break in the diet, such as the ingestion of candy, bread, cake, ice cream, plain milk, etc. Inasmuch as "stealing forbidden foods" is as prevalent among celiac patients as it is among diabetics, this "accidental" partaking of prohibited foods should be considered when there is a sudden recurrence of abnormal stools after a period of normalcy. It is most important to spot and to correct such a violation of diet because it tends to set back the total course of the cure. The second cause of a sudden episode of loose stools is infection. Although this may occur with a severe upper respiratory infection, usually it is associated with milder upper respiratory infections in which there is low-grade fever and minimal signs of coryza or injection of the pharynx. Loose stools may also be caused by other parenteral infections, such as furunculosis, etc. In the average case loose stools associated with infections will occur primarily during the first 3 to 6 months of treatment. It is interesting to point out, furthermore, that the loose stools caused by infections usually will not be foul nor will they be associated with psychic setbacks—two characteristics that almost always accompany episodes of loose stools precipitated by a break in the diet.

Usually after a period of from 3 to 6 months of rigid dieting, the child no longer reacts to infections with episodes of loose stools, and he has developed an appearance of rugged health. If the child is maintained on a strict carbohydrate specific diet, he will gain and grow remarkably well and be completely healthy and happy. After a year on the diet, bread, cereal and crackers may be eaten without risk. After another week or two, potato is added, and after three months, whole milk may be included. In the majority of cases, full health and activity continue, and at about 18 months after the diet has been instituted, all restrictions may be removed, and no diarrhea or ill health will result. In a few cases the addition of bread, cereal and potato at the end of a year will be followed, in a few weeks or a month, by a recurrence of loose stools. These cases must be considered insufficiently dieted and must be returned to the carbohydrate specific diet for an additional period of about three months. After this, no setback occurs when bread, cereal and potato are added to the diet.

It may well be asked why a period of a full year on the carbohydrate specific diet is prescribed. Although we recognize that there may be some cases that could tolerate a full diet sooner, we never have felt it wise to use a shorter period because of the risk of relapse involved.

There is a special case which deserves attention. This is the child who, for one reason or another—usually compulsive neurotic tendencies on the part of the parents—has frequent breaks in the diet. In these children short periods of loose stools will occur frequently as lapses in the diet take place. Such children will grow and gain normally but will not show satisfactory behavioral improvement. In such cases, when bread, cereal and potato are introduced at the end of a year, loose stools are very apt to occur. This may continue for many years. We have treated two girls, now in their twenties, who, during the dietary period of childhood, had persistent lapses and consequent attacks of loose stools. This continued until their late teens when they returned for treatment because the diarrheal attacks interfered with their normal activities. After the second period of treatment, which they followed rigidly, they became completely free from diarrhea.

In discussing the source of celiac disease under proper treatment, we must pay some attention to "catastrophe" or "crisis" because it is an occurrence described by other authors. When a case of celiac disease is treated correctly by a carbohydrate specific diet and breaks in the diet do not occur, "crises" never will take place, no matter how severe the case may have been initially. In all our experience we have seen no "crises" such as Heubner,[248] Howland,[261] Fanconi,[165] Andersen,[10] and others describe where there is severe watery diarrhea resulting in dehydration, electrolyte loss and shock, and where hospitalization for intravenous therapy has been necessitated. Not even in those cases just starting treatment, where an intervening infection may have resulted in very frequent, soft, or watery stools for a short period, have we ever seen dehydration requiring any sort of parenteral fluid, much less hospitalization, nor any case which could be considered grave or dangerous. In short, we state categorically that during treatment by a carbohydrate specific diet, "crises" will not occur.

The later course of the child treated by means of the carbohydrate specific diet is excellent. After a full diet has been achieved, there are no restrictions and no recurrence of even short periods of loose stools. The general level of health, growth and development is excellent. As a matter of fact, we have the distinct impression that it is above average and that these children tend to be bigger, stronger and more resistant to the minor illnesses of childhood than children who never have had celiac disease. Perhaps a reason for this is that the celiac patient, because of his therapeutic diet, never develops much of an appetite for sweets and bread and tends toward a higher protein intake than does the usual child.

PROGNOSIS

We may state categorically that the prognosis of celiac disease, when treated by means of a carbohydrate specific diet, is excellent from the standpoints of mortality, morbidity and cure. When treated in this fashion, the only cause of death could be the development of some disease other than celiac disease. Under this therapy, after the first few months, the general health will be excellent and, without a record of the history, the child will be indistinguishable from normal children. If the therapy is carried out adequately, most cases will have to follow no dietary restrictions, will be healthy, and will have normal stools by the end of 18 months. There are occasional cases that have been guilty of dietary lapses that may require a longer period, but even these will respond in a maximum of from 2 to 3 years. It must be stressed here that we do not consider as cured those cases which some authors report in which the child on a full diet seems to be normal aside from an occasional bout of diarrhea. This type of result does not occur when treatment by means of a carbohydrate specific diet is used. In short, by our method mortality is zero, and complete cure is effected in 18 months. It should be added that with this treatment, either during the course of the disease or afterward, there is no stunting of growth, no underweight, no edema, no anemia, and no forms of avitaminoses such as rickets, scurvy, beriberi, xerophthalmia, or pellagra.

ANALYSIS OF CASES

Over a period of some 25 years we have seen 603 children in whom the diagnosis of celiac disease was made. Of this total, 233 were not seen frequently enough or for a sufficiently long period to evaluate either the therapy or the results. Of this number 90 cases were seen only once as consultations referred to us by other physicians. The 143 remainder were seen only a few times for a period of less than 3 months each, before being lost track of for various reasons. (See Table 1.)

Of the 370 cases adequately followed over a period of some length, 270, or 73 per cent, were cured; 89, or 24 per cent, are recent cases still being treated and are on the road to cure; 8, or 2.2 per cent, were not cured; and 3, or 0.8 per cent, died. Cured cases are here considered as those patients who tolerate a full normal diet at the end of an arbitrarily established period of 3 years. (See Table 2.)

TABLE 1

TOTAL NUMBER OF CASES—603

Male	333 (55 per cent)
Female	270 (45 per cent)
Treated	370
Seen only briefly	233

Of 233 cases seen too briefly to evaluate:

90 were seen only once as consultations referred to us by other physicians

143 were seen only a few times during a short period and were lost track of for various reasons

TABLE 2

TOTAL NUMBER OF CASES TREATED—370

	Number	Per Cent
Cured	270	73
Under treatment	89	24
Not cured	8	2.2
Died	3	0.8

Data as to the length of time between onset of the disease and first treatment by us is available for 232 cases. In many of these cases diagnosis was made before we saw the patients. (See Table 3.)

Cases not cured are those patients who were unable to take a full diet at the end of 3 years. Of these 8 failures, 4 patients refused to follow the diet strictly and persistently;

1 was finally cured after 4½ years; 1 was cured after 6 years; 1 suffered a relapse after asthma; and 1, who had regularly eaten potatoes from the early months of treatment, now has loose stools whenever excessive amounts of candy or cake are eaten. (See Table 4.)

TABLE 3

TIME BETWEEN ONSET AND FIRST TREATMENT BY US—232 CASES

Under 3 months	53	2 to 3 years	13
3 to 6 months	38	3 to 4 years	15
6 months to 1 year	47	4 to 6 years	10
1 to 2 years	53	6 to 7½ years	3

TABLE 4

TOTAL NUMBER NOT CURED—8

Diet not followed	4
Cured after 4½ years	1
Cured after 6 years	1
Relapse after asthma	1
Occasional loose stools	1

The summary of those patients who died is as follows:

1. E. G. was first seen on December 7, 1925, at 16½ months of age, and hospitalized; gained 1½ pounds in first week, then acquired a ward infection of influenza and died of bronchopneumonia at the end of the second week of observation, December 20, 1925, having been under observation only 13 days.

2. J. B., child of a physician, first seen on October 18, 1943, at 3½ months, died 9 weeks later of acute tracheobronchitis, December 25, 1943, after a few days illness.

3. R. B. was first seen on August 27, 1937, at 15 months of age. He grew 6¼ inches and gained 7 pounds in the next 15 months. At the age of 31 months he became ill with a pulmonary infection and died after 4 weeks, January 30, 1939, of empyema, pericarditis with effusion, and extensive pneumonia.

Of the cured cases, the age of onset of the disease was ascertained for 237 patients, as shown in Table 5.

TABLE 5

AGE OF ONSET, CURED CASES—237

	Number	Per Cent
Onset at birth	38	16
2 days to 6 months	59	25
6 to 12 months	89	37.6
1 to 2 years	38	16
2 to 4 years	11	4.6
Over 4 years	2	.8

The time at which diarrhea was completely controlled is known for 189 of the cured cases. (See Table 6.)

TABLE 6

TIME OF CONTROL OF DIARRHEA—189 CASES

	Number	Per Cent
Within 1 month	36	19
2 to 5 months	88	46
6 to 10 months	51	27
11 to 14 months	11	6
15 to 24 months	3	2

Our figures showing the length of time between the beginning of treatment and toleration of a full diet are based on 231 cases, as shown in Table 7.

TABLE 7

DURATION OF TREATMENT BEFORE TOLERATION OF
FULL DIET—231 CASES

	Number	Per Cent
Less than 1 year	27	11.7
12 to 18 months	104	45
18 to 24 months	58	25.1
24 to 30 months	24	10.4
30 to 36 months	7	3
36 to 42 months	7	3
42 months to 6 years	4	1.8

All cases whenever seen were carefully checked, not only as to whether the diet given was as directed but also whether any additional substances such as candy, cake, or bread had been ingested even in minute amounts. In a large number of these cases it was definitely shown that ordinary forms of carbohydrates given in small amounts produced diarrhea. This statement is based on the frequent observation that a child with celiac disease treated by means of the specific carbohydrate diet for an adequate time, who had formed stools, who was eating and growing well, had suddenly developed diarrhea for a short period. Upon investigation it was learned that a very small piece of bread, a single lollypop, a teaspoon of ice cream, or a cookie had preceded the diarrhea by a period of from 6 to 24 hours.

It was also noted in this series that soon after the institution of the specific carbohydrate diet the first improvement noted was in the behavior and the disposition of the child.

The stools become less frequent and more formed, and a diuresis may occur. If there has been a clinical edema, this disappears with concomitant weight loss.

The excellent results shown in these figures indicate that patients with the disease can be cured completely and that they will not relapse or show residual physical defects. The proper treatment for celiac disease is clearly shown to be the specific carbohydrate diet described above.

TABLE 8. FAMILIAL INCIDENCE

Fanconi	Sisters	2
	Identical twins	2
	Parents, brothers or sisters who suffered from chronic intestinal disturbance	6
Feer	Sisters	2
Hablützel and Weber	Twins	2
Hess	Sisters	
Lehndorff·and Mautner	Cousins	
	Nephews	
Sauer	Cousins	4
	Twins	2
Haas	Sisters (2 pair)	4
	Cousins (5 pair)	10
	Second cousins	4
	Twins, identical (1 pair)	2
	Twins (1 pair)	2
	Uncle	1

Made up as follows:

Shirley B. ....Had an older sister who died from the disease two years before the present patient was born
Rita G. ....Had a cousin five years younger than she
Mortimer R. ....Had a cousin, Robert S.; had a second cousin, Philip R.; had an uncle, Mr. P.
L. twins (identical) ...Both affected
Vivian K. ....Had a cousin, Martin B., two and a half years younger
Caroline B. ....Had a sister three years older
Eleanore S. ....Had a cousin, Eleanore S., five years older
Marvin L. ....Had a cousin, Mary H.
Sally L. ....Had two second cousins, Stuart B. and Ralph B. (brothers)
Barbara H. ....One of twins; the other died before coming under treatment

TABLE 9. SYMPTOMS, ESPECIALLY OF AVITAMINOSIS (in 8 Cases)

	Rosiland L.	Daniel S.	Joan R.	Rose S.	Rita G.	Robert S.	Mortimer R.
Sex	F	M	F	F	F	M	M
Age (first seen)	15 months	3 years	17 months	4¼ years	12 months	13½ months	23 months
Weight	18-10	19	15-4	23½	12-6	13-8	20
Length	76 cm.	84 cm.	76 cm.	89 cm.	67 cm.	72 cm.	74 cm.
Sweating	X	X	X		X	X	X
Edema	X–	X	X	X	X	—	X
Erythema	—	—	X	X	X	X	X
Urticaria	—	—	X	X	X	X	X
Photophobia	—	X	X	X	X	X	X
Hyperthesia	X	X	X	X	X	X	X
Stomatitis	X	X	X	X	X	X	X
Paresis	—	X	X	X–	X	—	X
Anorexia	X – – –	X	X	X	X	—	X
Voracious Appetite						X	
Vomiting	X – –	X	X	X	X	X–	X
Diarrhea	X	X–	X	X	X	X–	X
Stools	Loose Yellow	Bulky Gray	Irreg. Bulky	Gray Bulky		Gray Bulky	Gray Bulky
Irritable	X	X	X	X	X	X	X
Pallor	X	X	X	X	X	X	X
Urine	—	Indic.	Indic.	Gran Casts	—	—	Gran Casts
Dentition @	2 yrs. 14		2 yrs. 16		2 yrs. 14	2 yrs. 12	

19

An Etiologic Hypothesis

The question of etiology is of paramount importance in celiac disease, inasmuch as it is the determining factor in treatment. At the outset it is necessary to stress the point that the etiology is not known, and that any discussion must perforce be hypothetical. However, any theories considered must be based on observed clinical facts and must be adequately specific so as to permit of an approach to investigation and to supply a rationale to guide thinking in relation to therapy.

Views of etiology such as "a postulated congenital weakness," a "constitutional defect," or "faulty absorption of nutritional elements" contain no concrete ideas which aid either in investigation or in treatment. For example, because of the steatorrhea associated with celiac disease, it has been stated that the etiology lies in some constitutional weakness of fat absorption. This point of view is obviously incorrect, since the disease continues with or without steatorrhea and is not improved or cured by restricting or modifying the fat intake of the patient. Such a view leads not only to incorrect modes of therapy but also to improper and wasteful lines of investigation. As a result of this etiologic theory, a tremendous amount of work has been done on stool-fat excretion, fat balances, vitamin A absorption, etc. All of this investigation has further elucidated only the fact that fat absorption is poor during the severe diarrheal phase of the disease, a conclusion which can be ascertained readily by a gross examination of the stools and a glance at the patient. Another etiologic theory states that since, in the severe phase, the oral blood sugar curve is flat and the intravenous normal,

and since the duodenal enzymes which act to split carbohydrates are present, the fault lies in the absorption and
not in the splitting of the carbohydrates. This is postulation-
ally attributed to a constitutional defect in the phosphorylation mechanism. Such a theory is extremely vague and
explains little. One of the earliest theories of etiology was
presented by Herter. As a result of his findings of a gram-
positive bacillus in the stools of some cases of celiac disease,
Herter concluded that the disease was an infectious one. No
investigator, however, has shown epidemiologic evidence to
substantiate this theory.

We have hypothecated an etiology of celiac disease based
upon observed clinical facts. We emphasize, however, that
this etiology must be considered completely hypothetical
until such time as the ideas in it may be verified by suitable
experimental means. Our hypothesis is that there is some
mechanism in the intestinal tract of the celiac sufferer which
converts polysaccharides into substances that are irritating
to the intestinal tract. These irritants cause such rapid
motility of the gut that absorption is interfered with and
malnutrition results. We base this view on facts which we
have observed in treating over 600 cases of celiac disease.
When all carbohydrates except those that are found in fruits,
vegetables and protein milk are withdrawn from the diet, the
diarrhea disappears, and the nutrition improves. If, however,
during the period of normal intestinal activity and nutrition
that follows soon after the institution of the proper diet, the
patient ingests even a small amount of bread, cookie, cake,
candy, sugar, plain milk, potato, or any other food containing polysaccharides, a loose or watery stool will occur within
from 6 to 18 hours. The patient will return to normalcy in
intestinal activity and nutrition if no more of the offending
foods are fed. We have observed, furthermore, that this cycle
may be repeated many times in the same individual, although
if done frequently and persistently enough, it will result in
a more prolonged period of diarrhea until intestinal activity

and nutrition can be restored to normalcy by the use of the "carbohydrate specific" diet.

In considering the cause of these observed facts, one is struck by the common denominator which exists in the foodstuffs which are not followed by diarrhea and in those which precipitate it. The common factor of the foods in the "carbohydrate specific" diet is that they contain a high proportion of such monosaccharides as glucose and levulose and only a small amount of the other sugars. The common factor of the foods that precipitate diarrhea is that they contain large proportions of such polysaccharides as lactose, sucrose, dextrins and starch. We conclude, therefore, that it is the polysaccharides which cause the diarrheal state, and that their elimination, as completely as possible, will· result in early cessation of diarrhea. This conclusion seems to be supported in clinical practise in cases where there is only partial elimination of polysaccharides, such as a diet which is a duplicate of the one we use except for such an apparently minor difference as the use of plain instead of protein milk. In such cases, a partial control with only a minimum of diarrhea and interference with nutrition may be achieved and may be continued for years. When protein milk is substituted for plain milk, the condition is corrected quickly and completely. It would be interesting to observe the results of therapy in a series of hospitalized cases treated by a synthetic diet in which proteins and fats were unrestricted in quantity or in kind, but in which carbohydrates were limited only to pure glucose or levulose. In a series of about a dozen cases in our own private practise, we fed pure levulose to the patients while they were on the "carbohydrate specific" diet with no resultant diarrhea. We performed this experiment in cases which we knew to be very sensitive to polysaccharides. We gave a number of such patients a teaspoonful of pure levulose three times a day for from 2 to 3 weeks and observed no diarrhea or other adverse clinical symptoms.

The next question to consider in developing our etiologic

hypothesis is why the polysaccharides are a cause of diarrhea. It cannot be that they form concentrated solutions which are irritant per se, since even a small amount will incite diarrhea. Furthermore, polysaccharides are not irritating to tissues—either mucous or smooth muscle—unless in very high concentration. Therefore, we have concluded that the polysaccharides are converted in the intestine into other irritant substances. This conversion might be performed through abnormality of a gut enzyme system or it might be carried out by a micro-organism such as the unusual *B. bifidis* or *B. infantilis* of Herter or even by the common *B. coli* in a form that possesses abnormal metabolism. However, whether the process is carried out by an enzyme system or by a micro-organism, it could be the same. Instead of first splitting the polysaccharide into two molecules which can then undergo normal metabolic processes, the polysaccharide is synthesized into a substance such as a long-chain fatty acid or an anthroquinone which then acts as a direct irritant to the smooth muscle of the intestines. Inasmuch as a small amount of polysaccharide produces, within 6 to 18 hours, a diarrhea that may last for a number of days, we have tended to lean to the theory that the irritant produced from the synthesis of the polysaccharide may be one of the anthroquinones.

Before discussing the possible synthesis of such an anthroquinone in greater detail, let us say that we tend to believe that the causative agent of such a synthesis is a micro-organism rather than an altered enzyme system. Our belief is based on the following reasoning. If polysaccharides are withheld from the diet for a sufficiently long time, they may then be fed without adverse effects. This hints that a strain of micro-organism that may be present in the intestine disappears or alters its characteristics when it is deprived of a polysaccharide substrate for a sufficiently long time. In normal infants during the neonatal period, an excess of carbohydrate in the formula will result in loose stools which may be corrected by a reduction in carbohydrate. This fact, combined with Herter's finding of *B. bifidis* and *B. infantilis* in the stools of neonatal normal infants, as well as in older children suffering from celiac disease, seems to be not without significance. There are various substances, e.g., sulfonamides, penicillin, liver extract, which interfere with or change bacterial metabolism. Some of these substances will also alter the course of celiac disease at least temporarily. It is also interesting to note here that starvation of the celiac patient during the diarrheal phase will result in cessation of the diarrhea which will start again when food is given. Furthermore, parenteral infection in a celiac case will be accompanied by diarrhea. One might inquire here, parenthetically, why the fact that parenteral infection in otherwise normal children is accompanied by diarrhea has not been investigated more critically.

Given a hypothesis that the diarrhea of celiac disease is caused by an anthroquinone irritant produced by a microorganism from a polysaccharide substrate, the following facts make the theory plausible.

A. Sterochemically, the formation of two benzene rings connected by carbon atoms as in anthroquinone is not too difficult to advance when one considers that a disaccharide is composed of two 6-carbon atom chains which also assume a cyclic structure, or even more so when anthroquinone is formed by the chemist from a benzol benzoic acid.

B. Bacterium is capable of forming cellulose and dextran from a monosaccharide substrate.

C. A mold, penicillium glaucus, produces physion (4,5,7 trihydroxy 2 methyl anthroquinone) from a glucose substrate.

D. The action of the anthroquinone cathartics (the emodine purgatives) is similar to the diarrhea observed in celiac disease, and the action of large doses of phenolphthalein results in repeated evacuations for from 3 to 4 days with urine excretion throughout the period, although only one dose be given.

E. It has been shown experimentally that the stimulating effect of emodine on smooth muscle may be blocked by atropine, and contrariwise physostigmine produces a celiac-like diarrhea in cats.

This theory delineates certain paths of investigation that might be profitably pursued:

1. Feeding celiac patients with synthetic monosaccharide diets and comparing them with patients who are fed the polysaccharides.

2. Investigation of active celiac cases for the presence in stool or urine of irritants such as the anthroquinones.

3. Animal experiments involving the feeding of filtrates from the stools of active celiac cases to observe the effect on the animals' gastro-intestinal tracts.

4. Bacteriologic investigations in which the isolation of organisms from the stools of celiac cases might reveal a metabolic defect of the bacteria.

Summary

1. The *Symptoms* of celiac disease will persist so long as polysaccharides (complex carbohydrates) are ingested and will disappear only if monosaccharides (simple carbohydrates) are used with the addition of protein and fats, the latter being well utilized if the polysaccharides are excluded from the diet. These observations are based on a clinical experience of 30 years and have been substantiated by laboratory investigation as well.

2. There is no symptom pathognomonic of celiac disease, and no laboratory procedure which can do more than add to the support of such a diagnosis.

3. There is a familial tendency to the disease.

4. The *Etiology* is still unknown.

5. Celiac is a disease and not a syndrome, since it responds regularly to a specific form of therapy.

6. The *Picture* of the disease may be the classical one of the literature (emaciation, stunting, large abdomen, irritability and malnutrition) or so slight as to escape notice for what it is (nutrition excellent).

7. The *Prognosis* is excellent under correct treatment.

8. The *Treatment* is definite, i.e., a diet from which polysaccharides (complex carbohydrates) are excluded so far as possible. Monosaccharides in all forms are well tolerated, and with their use any difficulty with fats disappears. This is the basis of the celiac diet; proteins in any form seem to be acceptable.

Bibliography

1. Adamson, A. C., and Lewes, D.: Proteolyzed beef, Brit. M. J. 2:370, 1944.
2. Adlersberg, D.: Fat and vitamin A absorption in sprue, New York State J. Med. 44:606, 1944.
3. Agerty, H. A.: Nutrition and diet in infants and children V; Special diets for abnormal states, Hahneman. Monthly 73:679, 1938.
4. Akerren, Y.: Over-curved nails in celiac disease, Nord. med. (Hygiea) 18:803, 1943.
5. Allibone, E. C.: Vitamin D complex and liver extract, Proc. Roy. Soc. Med. 39:700, 1946.
6. Allodi, A.: Chronic idiopathic steatorrhea; case, Arch. ital. mal. app. diger. 5:253, 1936.
7. Alloiteau, J.-J., and Jud, S.: Digestion and intestinal absorption in celiac disease, Arch. pédiat. 4:109, 1949.
8. Andersen, D. H.: Pancreatic enzymes in the duodenal juice in the celiac syndrome, Am. J. Dis. Child. 50:1418, 1935.
9. ——: Cystic fibrosis of the pancreas and its relation to celiac disease: a clinical and pathological study, Am. J. Dis. Child. 56:344, 1938.
10. ——: Cystic fibrosis of the pancreas, vitamin A deficiency, and bronchiectasis, J. Pediat. 15:763, 1939.
11. ——: "Celiac syndrome" *in* Brenneman's Practice of Pediatrics, Hagerstown, Md., Prior, 1941.
12. ——: Pancreatic enzymes in the duodenal juice in the celiac syndrome, Am. J. Dis. Child. 63:643, 1942.
13. ——: Celiac syndrome; determination of fat in feces; reliability of two chemical methods and of microscopic estimate, Am. J. Dis. Child. 69:221, 1945.
14. ——: Celiac syndrome; fecal excretion in congenital pancreatic deficiency at various age levels and with various diets; with discussion of optimal diet, Am. J. Dis. Child. 69:231, 1945.
15. ——: Celiac syndrome; dietary therapy for congenital pancreatic deficiency, Am. J. Dis. Child. 70:100, 1945.
16. ——: Relationship of celiac disease, starch intolerance, and steatorrhea, J. Pediat. 30:564, 1947.
17. Andersen, D. H., and Hodges, R. G.: Celiac syndrome;

genetics of cystic fibrosis of the pancreas with a consideration of etiology, Am. J. Dis. Child. 72:62, 1946.

18. Andersen, M.: Celiac disease, Hospitalstid. 79:434, 1936.

19. Anderson, A. G., and Lyall, A.: Two cases of fatty diarrhea (one of non-tropical sprue) with special reference to nitrogen metabolism, Quart. J. Med. 2:339, 1933.

20. Anslow, W. K., et al.: Studies in biochemistry of microorganisms, Miochem. J. 34:159, 1940.

21. Antonini, M., and Medda, E.: A case of celiac disease, Clin. pediat. mod. 18:44, 1936.

22. Aretaeus the Cappadocian: On the Causes and Symptoms of Chronic Diseases, London, The Sydenham Society, 1856.

23. Armstrong, M.: Celiac disease, Am. J. Dis. Child. 35:414, 1920.

24. Aron, H.: Fruit diet and sugar diet, Arch. f. Kinderh. 95:151, 1932.

25. Asher, C.: Infantilism with bony changes resembling rickets and calcification in kidneys, Arch. Dis. Childhood 11:311, 1936.

26. Ashley, J. N., et al.: Pigments of a glaucus series, Biochem. J. 33:1291, 1939.

27. Ayers, W. B., et al.: Fibrocystic disease of the pancreas; treatment by sympathetic denervation of the pancreas and presentation of a theory of neuroeffector mechanisms: preliminary report of five cases, J. A. M. A. 142:7, 1950.

28. Badenock, E., and Morris, M.: Carbohydrate metabolism; effect of insulin and of active pituitary extract. Quart. J. Med. 5:227, 1936.

29. Baggenstoss, A. H., et al.: The relationship of fibrocystic disease of the pancreas to a deficiency of secretin, Pediatrics 2:435, 1948.

30. Banu, G. H.: A case of celiac disease, Bull. soc. med. hop. Bucarest 6:35, 1924.

31. Barber, W. W.: Celiac disease, Am. J. Nursing 36:660, 1936.

32. Bargebuhr, H.: The Cause and Prognosis of Sufferers from Herter-Heubner's Infantilism, Göttingen, thesis, 1931.

33. Barling, B.: Two cases of idiopathic steatorrhea, Annual Rep. London Co. Council 4:143, 1935.

34. Barnes, B. C., et al.: The comparative absorption of vitamin A from a water-miscible and an oily preparation by normal human adults and patients with steatorrhea, J. Clin. Investigation 29:982, 1950.

35. Barta, L., and Vince, I.: Influence of adrenal cortex on sugar metabolism, Ann. pediat. 173:17, 1949.

36. Bartley, C. W.: Steatorrhea in family (possible relation to fibrocystic disease of pancreas), Brit. M. J. 1:1161, 1950.

37. Bassett, S. H., et al.: Metabolism in idiopathic steatorrhea: influence of dietary and other factors on lipid and mineral balance, J. Clin. Investigation 18:101, 1939.

38. ——: Metabolism in idiopathic steatorrhea; effect of liver extract and vitamin D on calcium, phosphorus, nitrogen, and lipid balances, J. Clin. Investigation 18:121, 1939.

39. Bauer, E. L.: Celiac disease, Am. J. Dis. Child. 35:414, 1928.

40. Baumann, E. P.: Celiac disease, J. M. A. South Africa 1:255, 1927.

41. Baumann, T.: Action of Raw Fruit Diet on Children's Organisms, Berlin, 1936.

42. Baumann, W.: Value of raw milk in prevention of osteoporosis and scurvy following intestinal infantilism; three cases, Monatschr. f. Kinderh. 42:5, 1929.

43. Behrens, G.: A Case of Celiac Disease, Freiburg, thesis, 1930.

44. Bender, H. A.: Acute mastoiditis in celiac disease, J. Iowa M. Soc. 34:429, 1944.

45. Bennett, T. I.: Gee's disease, Lancet 2:739, 1934.

46. Bennett, T. I., and Hardwick, C.: Chronic jejuno-ileal insufficiency: pathogenesis of celiac disease, Lancet, 2:381, 1940.

47. Bennett, T. I., et al.: Idiopathic steatorrhea (Gee's disease) nutritional disturbances associated with tetany, osteomalacia, and anemia, Quart J. Med. 1:603, 1932.

48. Bensaude, R., et al.: Developmental disorders of digestive origin, Prat. méd. fr. 14:99, 1933.

49. Berheim-Karrer, M.: Intestinal infantilism, Rev. méd. de la Suisse Rom. 37:884, 1927.

50. Berney, D. E.: Celiac disease treated with unusual diet (Dennett), Pennsylvania M. J. 34:250, 1931.

51. Bessau, H.: Chronic intestinal insufficiency in childhood, Berlin klin. Wchnschr. 53:262, 1916.

52. Best, C. H., and Taylor, N. B.: The Physiological Basis of Medical Practice, ed. 3, Baltimore, Williams & Wilkins, 1943.

53. Bing, J. and Broager, G.: Effect of nicotinic acid on two patients with idiopathic steatorrhea, Acta med. Scandinav. 97:561, 1938.

54. Birutaviciene, A.: Intestinal infantilism, Medicina kaunas. 15:152, 1934.

55. Bischoff, G.: Effects of ingestion of bile acids on resorptive processes in intestinal canal in intestinal infantilism, Arch. f. Kinderh. 90:73, 1930.

56. Bjerkelund, C. J.: Symptomatic sprue; study of six verified cases, Acta med. Scandinav. 137:130, 1950.

57. Blackfan, K. D. (ed.) : Report of Committee on Growth and Development of Children, New York, Commonwealth Fund, 1932.
58. Blackfan, K. D., and May, C. D.: Inspissation of secretion, dilation of the ducts and acini, atrophy and fibrosis of the pancreas in infants: clinical note, J. Pediat. 13:627, 1938.
59. Blanchard, K.: Celiac disease and its treatment, J. M. Soc. New Jersey 27:222, 1930.
60. Blatt, M., et al.: Phenolphthalein tolerance in childhood, J. Pediat. 22:719, 1943.
61. Bloch, C. E.: Clinical and anatomical investigation of infantilism intestinalis (celiac disease, Samuel Gee), Acta paediat. Supp. 27:207, 1928.
62. ——: Intestinal infantilism as an avitaminosis, Norsk. mag. f. laegevidensk. 91:1055, 1930.
63. Bloch, H.: Celiac syndrome due to gastrointestinal allergy, Arch. Pediat. 66:54, 1949.
64. Bluhdorn, K.: Toward a knowledge of the chronic intestinal insufficiency of childhood, Monatschr. f. Kinderh. 21:433, 1921.
65. Bluhdorn, K., and Volkers, H.: Selected chapters concerning the diseases of the new-born, infants, and young children, Beitr. z. med. Klin. 1924.
66. Bolten, G. C.: Case of infantilism with manifest tetany, Geneesk. gids. 7:97, 1929.
67. Borchardt, L.: Concerning the definition and etiology of infantilism, Deutsch. Arch. f. klin. Med. 138:129, 1922.
68. ——: Intestinal infantilism and exophthalmic goiter as causes of essential differences in enzygotic twins, Ztschr. f. d. Ges. Anat. 16:123, 1931.
69. Bousser, J., and Robineaux, R.: Action of folic acid and liver extract in sprue, Sang. 20:472, 1949.
70. Boyd, J. D.: Therapeutic use of diets, J. Pediat. 8:234, 1936.
71. Brailsford, J. F.: Radiographic findings in idiopathic steatorrhea, Brit. J. Radiol. 16:283, 1943.
72. Bramwell, B.: A case of infantilism, Tr. Med.-Chir. Soc. Edinburgh 21:94, 1902.
73. ——: A case of infantilism, Clin. Stud. Edinburgh 1:57, 1903.
74. ——: Pancreatic infantilism, Tr. Med.-Chir. Soc. Edinburgh 23:162, 1904.
75. ——: Pancreatic infantilism, Clin. Stud. Edinburgh 2:68, 1903; 3:48, 1904.
76. ——: A case of pancreatic infantilism, Scott. Med. and Surg. J. 14:321, 1904.
77. ——: Pancreatic infantilism: clinical studies III, Edinburgh Med. 14:323, 1915.

78. Breese, B., and McCoord, A. B.: Vitamin A absorption, J. Pediat. 15:183, 1939.
79. Brennemann, J.: Celiac disease, M. Clin. North America 21:149, 1937.
80. Brewer, E. C.: A probable case of celiac disease, Arch. argent. de pediat. 9:294, 1938.
81. Bright, R.: Cases and observations connected with disease of the pancreas and duodenum, Med.-Chir. Trans. 18:1, 1833.
82. Brill, L.: New data on idiopathic steatorrhea, Acta clin. belg. 2:205, 1947.
83. Brøchner-Mortensen, K.: Serum iron in patients with hyperchromic anemia in idiopathic steatorrhea, Acta med. Scandinav. 113:362, 1943.
84. Brown, A.: Etiology and pathogenesis of celiac disease, Arch. Dis. Childhood 24:99, 1949.
85. Brown, C. A.: Etiology of chronic intestinal indigestion; chemical and physiological investigations, Am. J. Dis. Child. 30:303, 1925.
86. Brown, C. A., et al.: Etiology of chronic intestinal indigestion: clinical and bacteriological investigation, Am. J. Dis. Child. 30:603, 1925.
87. Brown, C. A., et al.: Effect of special high protein diets in chronic intestinal indigestion in children, Brit. J. Child. Dis. 19:113, 1922.
88. Brüning, F.: On the two hundredth birthday of a wonderchild, Tatung. der Ges. f. Kinderh. Jena 1921.
89. Bullrich, R. A.: Pancreatic infantilism (Bramwell's type), Rev. Asoc. méd. argent. 28:303, 1918.
90. Cacciapuoti, G. B.: Relation between dysthymia and abdominal disease; psycho-celiac syndrome, Cervello 23:129, 1947.
91. Cachera, R.: Celiac disease, Arch. d. mal. de l'app. digestif 38:668, 1949.
92. Caelius Aurelianus: Concerning acute diseases, Amsterdam, 1709.
93. Caffey, J. P.: Pediatric X-ray Diagnosis, Chicago, 1945.
94. Camacho Gamba, M. J.: Case of celiac disease, Rev. Fac. de med. Bogotá 7:219, 1938.
95. Camp, J. D., and Watkins, C. H.: Non-tropical sprue (chronic idiopathic steatorrhea), Proc. Staff Meet. Mayo Clin. 10:177, 1935.
96. Campanacci, D.: Chronic idiopathic steatorrhea associated with asthmatiform bronchiectasic bronchitis; therapeutic study of case, Minerva med. 2:57, 1937.
97. Caselli, E. G., et al.: Theory of achalasia: study apropos of case, Arch. argent. de pediat. 25:19, 1946.

98. Cautley, E.: Celiac disease, Trans. Med. Soc. London 1:700, 1919.
99. ——: Celiac disease, Arch. Pediat. 38:163, 1921.
100. Cavengt, S.: Digestive infantilism, Pediat. espan. 15:93, 1926.
101. ——: Intestinal infantilism: three cases, Mundo med. 14:958, 1932.
102. ——: Celiac disease, Arch. espan. de pediat. 19:21, 1935.
103. ——: Celiac disease, Arch. espan. de pediat. 19:90, 1935.
104. Cheadle, W. B.: On acholia, Lancet 81:149, 1903.
105. Cheinisse, E.: The malnutrition of digestive insufficiency of childhood, Semaine méd. 30:373, 1910.
106. Chesney, J., and McCord, A. B.: Vitamin A of serum following administration of haliver oil in normal children and in chronic steatorrhea, Proc. Soc. Exper. Biol. & Med. 31:887, 1934.
107. Chung, A. W.: The effect of oral feeding at different levels on the absorption of foodstuffs in infantile diarrhea, J. Pediat. 33:1, 1948.
108. Ciblis Aguirre, R., and Tetes, R. E.: Diagnosis and therapy; case, Arch. argent. de pediat. 4:344, 1933.
109. Ciblis Aguirre, R., et al.: Etiopathogenic and therapeutic study based on three cases, Arch. argent. de pediat. 17:237, 1942.
110. Clarke, C., and Hadfield, G.: Congenital pancreatic disease with infantilism, Quart. J. Med. 17:538, 1924.
111. Coleman, A. B.: Grid prodrome phenomenon in celiac disease; four cases, J. Pediat. 35:165, 1949.
112. Collins-Williams, C.: Idiopathic hypoparathyroidism with papilledema in a boy six years of age; report of a case associated with moniliasis and the celiac syndrome and a brief review of the literature, Pediatrics 5:998, 1950.
113. Comby, J.: Celiac disease, Arch. de méd. d. enf. 27:553, 1924.
114. Comfort, M. W., et al.: External pancreatic secretion as measured by secretin test in patients with idiopathic steatorrhea (non-tropical sprue), Gastroenterology 13:135, 1949.
115. Cordeiro Ferreira, and Brandao de Oliviera: Celiac disease with report of case, Lisboa méd. 16:239, 1939.
116. Cordier, V., and Dechaume, J.: Pluriglandular syndrome; infantilism, Lyon méd. 137:192, 1926.
117. Correa, O.: Analysis of pancreatic enzymes in infants and small children: dystrophy, seborrheic dermatitis, and celiac disease, Rev. chilena de pediat. 18:11, 1947.
118. Courtin, W.: Prognosis of intestinal infantilism, Monatschr. f. Kindehr. 58:39, 1933.

119. Courtney, A. B., and Mac Lachland, D. J.: Etiology of chronic intestinal indigestion, Am. J. Dis. Child. 30:603, 1925.
120. Crawford, T.: Causation of low blood-sugar curve, Quart. J. Med. 8:251, 1939.
121. Critchley, M.: Celiac infantilism; celiac rickets; latent tetany (case), Proc. Roy. Soc. Med. 25:1538, 1932.
122. Curry, F. S.: Chronic steatorrhea with tetany: case, Proc. Staff Meet. Mayo Clin. 7:501, 1932.
123. Cushny, A. R.: Pharmacology and Therapeutics, ed. 13, Philadelphia, Lea & Febiger, 1947.
124. Czerny, A., and Keller, A.: Nutrition of children, ed. 2. Leipzig and Vienna, Deuticke, 1923-1928.
125. Danielson, W. H., et al.: Intestinal absorption of vitamin A from oily and aqueous media in patients with the celiac syndrome, Pediatrics 3:645, 1949.
126. Davidson, L. S. P., and Fountain, J. R.: Incidence of sprue syndrome with some observations on natural history, Brit. M. J. 1:1157, 1950.
127. Davison, W. C.: Celiac disease: chronic intestinal indigestion, South. Med. & Surg. 97:78, 1935.
128. De Angelis, F.: Celiac disease, Pediatria 32:221, 1924.
129. Debenedetti, V.: Etiology of celiac disease, Pediatria 35:577, 1927.
130. De Elizalde, P., and White, F. E.: Celiac disease, Arch. argent. de pediat. 2:746, 1931.
131. De Langen, C. D.: Association of Simmonds' disease and Gee-Thaysen's disease, Nederl. tijdschr. v. geneesk. 81:2896, 1937.
132. De Murtas, C.: Celiac disease in infant; case, Riv. di clin. pediat. 28:473, 1930.
133. De Serio, N.: Pathogenesis of intestinal infantilism; case, Arch. radiol. 24:68, 1949.
134. De Takats, G., and Cuthbert, F. P.: Effects of celiac ganglionectomy on sugar tolerance, Am. J. Physiol. 102:527, 1933.
135. De Toni, G.: Chronic colonopathies of children; colonopathies due to megacolon, dolichocolon, celiac disease, and colonic interposition, Rev. frse. de pédiat. 15:1, 1939.
136. De Ville, P. M., and Meyers, B.: Cured celiac disease:achondroplasia, Proc. Roy. Soc. Med. London 26:1351, 1933.
137. Dicke, W. K.: Intestinal infantilism and pseudo pernicious anemia, Maandschr. v. Kindergeneesk. 5:406, 1936.
138. Dieckhoff, J.: Pathogenesis and therapy of celiac disease, Arch. Kinderh. 138:161, 1950.
139. Di Sant' Agnese, P. E. A., and Andersen, D. H.: Celiac syndrome: chemotherapy in infections of the respiratory

tract associated with cystic fibrosis of the pancreas: observations with penicillin and drugs of the sulfonamide group, with special reference to penicillin aerosol, Am. J. Dis. Child. 72:17, 1946.

140. ——: Paper delivered before American Academy of Pediatrics, 1950.

141. Doudoroff, M.: The utilization and synthesis of sucrose and related compounds by some microorganisms, Fed. Proc. 4:241, 1948.

142. Drury, H. C.: The celiac affection, Dublin J. M. Sc. 135:241, 1913.

143. ——: Discussion, sprue and celiac disease, Tr. Roy. Soc. of Trop. Med. & Hyg. 17:11, 1924.

144. Duarte, A.: Celiac disease, J. pediat. Rio de Janeiro 4:183, 1937.

145. Dubois, R.: Clinical and Physiopathological Aspects of Celiac Disease, Paris, 1939.

146. Dunn, C. H.: Some studies on sugar in infant feeding, Arch. Pediat. 32:372, 1915.

147. Dyson, R. E.: Celiac disease in children, Journal Lancet 64:40, 1944.

148. Eaton, P. J.: Two cases of pancreatic infantilism, Brit. M. J. 2735:1162, 1913.

149. Eaton, P. J., and Woods, E. B.: Low fats and high proteins in infant feeding, Tr. Am. Pediat. Soc. 26:166, 1914.

150. Ebbs, J. H., et al.: Etiologic factors in celiac disease, Am. J. Dis. Child. 79:936, 1950.

151. Eckert, H.: Concerning intestinal infantilism (celiac disease), Berlin klin. Wchnschr. 49:1635, 1912.

152. Eddy, W. H.: The Nutritive Value of the Banana, New York, 1933.

153. Edgren, M.: Cases of so-called intestinal indigestion, in clillaeläk. sällsk. handl. 72:440, 1930.

154. Einhorn, M.: Celiac disease, M. J. & Rec. 138:466, 1933.

155. Elias, H., and Schachter, M.: Mental bearing of children with celiac disease, Progrès méd.: 286, 1934.

156. Elias, H., et al.: Contribution to a clinical study of celiac disease, Progrès méd. 2:1553, 1933.

157. Elias, H., et al.: Clinical study of Gee-Herter-Heubner's disease, Rev. stiint. med. 22:812, 1933.

158. Elvehjem, C. A., and Krahl, W. H.: Imbalance and dietary interrelationship in nutrition, J. A. M. A. 135:279, 1947.

159. Emery, J. L.: Carbohydrate metabolism in celiac disease, Arch. Dis. Childhood 22:41, 1947.

160. ——: Cold sweating, hypoglycemia, and carbohydrate insufficiency with particular reference to celiac disease, Arch. Dis. Childhood 22:34, 1947.

161. Emslie, C.: A case of infantilism, Proc. Roy. Soc. Med. 13:61, 1919-1920.
162. Ernberg, H.: Case of intestinal infantilism with hemorrhage, Hygiea Stockh. 88:725, 1926.
163. ——: Discussion on celiac disease, Jahrb. f. Kinderh. 130: 349, 1931.
164. ——: Case of intestinal infantilism treated with bananas, Acta paediat. 14:240, 1932.
165. Escardo, F.: Celiac Disease; Dietary Regimen Without Milk, Buenos Aires, Gleizer, 1933.
166. Evans, P. R.: Celiac disease with unusual features, Proc. Roy. Soc. Med. London 28:154, 1934-1935.
167. Evensen, O. K.: Gee-Herter's disease: new case from medical division A of Rikshospital, Norsk. mag. f. laegevidensk, 97:830, 1936.
168. Fabre, G.: Contribution to the Study of Celiac Disease, Paris, LeGrand, 1927.
169. Fabrizio, A.: Gee's disease, Rinasc. med. 11:585, 1934.
170. Fanconi, G.: Herter's infantilism; chemism and hematology, Monatschr. f. Kinderh. 37:454, 1927.
171. ——: Intestinal Infantilism and Similar Types of Chronic Nutritional Disorders, Basel, Karger, 1928.
172. ——: Chronic digestive disturbances in children; treatment with fruit and vegetable diet, Schweiz. med. Wchnschr. 58:789, 1928.
173. ——: Fruit diet in acute digestive disturbances of children, Acta Paediat. 11:380, 1930.
174. ——: Further experiences with fruit and vegetable diet in intestinal infantilism, Klin. Wchnschr. 9:553, 1930.
175. ——: Herter's infantilism, Maandschr. f. Kindergeneesk. 7:135, 1938.
176. ——: Celiac disease, Deutsch. med. Wchnschr. 64:1565; 1607, 1938.
177. Fanconi, G., et al.: Congenital cystic pancreatic fibromatosis and bronchiectasis, Wien. med. Wchnschr. 86:753, 1936.
178. Farber, S.: Pancreatic insufficiency and celiac syndrome, New England J. Med. 229:653; 682, 1943.
179. ——: Pancreatic function and disease in early life: pathologic changes associated with pancreatic insufficiency in early life, Arch. Path. 37:238, 1944.
180. Farber, S., et al.: Pancreatic disease and function in early life: pancreatic enzyme activity and celiac syndrome, J. Clin. Investigation, 22:827, 1943.
181. Farber, S., and Maddock, C. L.: The relation of the pancreas to the celiac syndrome, Am. J. Path. 17:445, 1941.
182. Feissly, R.: Physiopathology; study based on observation of

thirty cases of steatorrhea, Schweiz. med. Wchnschr. 68:70, 1938.

183. Fildes, P.: The production of indole by suspensions of B. coli, Biochem. J. 32:1600, 1938.

184. Fiori, P.: Gaseous Infections; Clinical, Bacteriological, Experimental, and Anatamo-pathological Considerations, Bologna, 1920.

185. Fleming, G. B., and Hutchinson, H. S.: A study of metabolism in the undernourished infant, Quart. J. Med. 17:339, 1923-1924.

186. Flesch, H.: Celiac disease, Orvosi netil. 75:503, 1931.

187. ——: Grave case of celiac disease, Kinderärtzl. Praxis. 2:494, 1931.

188. Ford, F. J.: Metabolism of healing in celiac rickets, Arch. Dis. Childhood 8:355, 1933.

189. Forsyth, D.: Celiac disease or boric acid poisoning? Lancet 2:728, 1919.

190. Fox, H. J.: Proteolytic activity in vitro at neutral reaction of gastric juice from patient with sprue, J. Clin. Investigation 28:678, 1949.

191. ——: Absorption of unemulsified and emulsified vitamin A in sprue, J. Lab. and Clin. Med. 34:1140, 1949.

192. ——: Sucral absorption in sprue, J. Lab. & Clin. Med. 35:622, 1950.

193. Frankel, B., and Elias, H.: Transition of chronic dyspepsia to celiac disease, Bull. Soc. pédiat. de Paris 30:381, 1932.

194. Frazer, A. C.: Fat metabolism and sprue syndrome, Brit. M. J. 2:769, 1949.

195. Freeman, R.: The intestinal infantilism of Herter, Am. J. Dis. Child. 2:332, 1911.

196. ——: Celiac disease, Internat. Clin. 3:195, 1923.

197. Freise, R., and Jahr, M.: Pathogenesis of Herter's infantilism, Jahrb. f. Kinderh. 110:205, 1925.

198. Freise, R., and Walenta, E.: Animal experiments on pathogenesis, Monatschr. f. Kinderh. 50:1, 1931.

199. Fuks, D., and Waisdein, S.: Therapy of celiac disease, Arch. am. de med. 12:64, 1936.

200. Freiericksen, C.: Quantitative investigation of resorption of A vitamin in case of celiac; hypovitaminosis A, Acta paediat. 18:377, 1936.

201. Fullerton, H. W., and Innes, J. A.: Idiopathic steatorrhea: case with multiple nutritional deficiencies, Lancet 2:790, 1936.

202. Gardiner, H. H.: Two cases of celiac infantilism, Proc. Roy. Soc. Med. London 22:69, 1928-1929.

203. Garrod, A. E., and Hertley, W. H.: Congenital familiary steatorrhea, Quart. J. Med. 6:242, 1912.

204. Gasbarrini, A.: Celiac-biliary syndrome due to primary adenocarcinoma of body of pancreas, Policlinica (sez. prat.) 56:1309, 1949.
205. Gee, S.: On the celiac affection, St. Barth. Hosp. Rep. 24:17, 1888.
206. Geill, T.: Non-tropical sprue (Gee's disease) case, Hospitalstid. 75:705, 1932.
207. Gelfand, M.: Celiac disease in tropical Africa, Tr. Roy. Soc. Trop. Med. & Hyg. 41:109, 1947.
208. Gerstenberger, H. J.: Preventive infant feeding, Am. J. Public Health 13:185, 1923.
209. Gianelli, C.: Celiac disease, Arch. de pediat. d. Uruguay 8:496, 1937.
210. Gibbons, R. A.: On the celiac affection in children, Edinburgh M. J. 35:321, 1889.
211. Gibbs, G. E.: Effect of pancreatin on plasma vitamin A curves in celiac syndrome (and cystic fibrosis of pancreas), Pediatrics 6:593, 1950.
212. Giffin, H. Z., et al.: Sub-acute combined degeneration of spinal cord unassociated with pernicious anemia, with note on neurologic changes that sometimes occur with sprue, non-tropical sprue, or idiopathic steatorrhea, Tr. A. Am. Physicians 51:240, 1936.
213. Gilbert, R., and Babaiantz, L.: Roentgen semeiology of intestinal infantilism, J. de radiol. et d'électrol. 18:381, 1934.
214. Giraud, P., and Astier, P.: Megadolichocolon with arrested development in child three years old; differential diagnosis of celiac disease, Bull. Soc. pédiat. de Paris 30:468, 1932.
215. Gjørup, E.: Case of celiac disease, Hospitalstid 74:1205, 1931.
216. ——: A case of severe diarrhea of pancreatic origin in a ten year old child, Acta paediat. 15:82, 1933-1934.
217. Glynn, L. E., and Rosenheim, M. L.: Mesenteric chyladenectasis with steatorrhea and features of Addison's disease (case), J. Path. and Bact. 47:285, 1938.
218. Goldberger, I. H.: Celiac disease, Arch. Pediat. 41:352, 1924.
219. Golden, R.: Abnormalities of the small intestine in nutritional disturbances, Radiology 36:262, 1941.
220. Gonce, J. E.: Steatorrhea in infants and children, Proc. Interst. Postgrad. M. A. North America, 1942, 222, 1943.
221. Gonzales Alvarez, F.: Clinical histories, Arch. argent. de pediat. 3:440; 503, 1932.
222. ——: Celiac disease, Arch. argent. de pediat. 3:580; 654; 732, 1932.

223. Gonzalves Carneiro, M.: Fruit treatment of bacillary dysentery and of acute and chronic diarrheal affections of children older than one year, Arch. ped. portug. 4:309, 1932.
224. Göttche, O.: Intestinal infantilism, Jahrb. f. Kinderh. 111:81, 1926.
225. Goubau, F.: Intestinal infantilism, Geneesk. tijdschr. v. Belgie 4:418, 1913.
226. Graves, L. G.: Food in Health and Disease, New York, Macmillan, 1932.
227. Greenberg, J.: Attempt to reproduce celiac disease experimentally in young animals by excluding external pancreatic secretion from intestine, Yale J. Biol. & Med. 6:121, 1933.
228. Griffith, J. P. C.: Chronic intestinal indigestion in early life, Arch. Pediat. 28:324, 1911.
229. Griffith, J. P. C., and Mitchell, A. G.: The Diseases of Infants and Children, ed. 2, Philadelphia, Saunders, 1937.
230. Gross, O.: Diseases of the Spleen, Liver, Gallbladder, and Pancreas, Vienna, Springer, 1920.
231. Gull, W.: Fatty stools from disease of the mesenteric glands, Guy's Hosp. Rep. 1:369, 1855.
232. Gurnie, G. W.: Chronic intestinal indigestion in infants and young children, Cleveland M. & S. Reporter 19:35, 1911.
233. Haas, S. V.: Value of banana in treatment of celiac disease, Am. J. Dis. Child. 28:421, 1924.
234. ——: Beriberi in late infancy; result of celiac disease, Arch. Pediat. 46:467, 1929.
235. ——: Specific treatment and cure without nutritional relapse, J. A. M. A. 99:448, 1932.
236. ——: Celiac disease and its ultimate prognosis, J. Pediat. 13:390, 1938.
237. Haas, S. V., and Haas, M. P.: Diagnosis and treatment of celiac disease: report of 603 cases, Postgrad. Med. 7:239, 1950.
238. Hablützel-Weber: Concerning Intestinal Infantilism and the Fate of Its Victims, Inaug. Diss. Zurich, 1923.
239. Haex, A. J. C.: Intestinal infantilism: case, Monatschr. f. Kindergeneesk. 5:174, 1936.
240. Hallez, G. L.: Herter's infantilism, Medecine 11:626, 1930.
241. Hanes, F. M., and McBryde, A.: Identity of sprue, nontropical sprue, and celiac disease, Arch. Int. Med. 58:1, 1936.
242. Hans, S. F.: Pelvic contraction due to idiopathic steatorrhea, J. Obst. Gyn. Brit. Empire 54:663, 1947.

243. Hardwick, C.: Congenital steatorrhea with congenital morbus cordis, Proc. Roy. Soc. Med. 32:319, 1939.
244. ——: Prognosis; review of 73 cases, Arch. Dis. Childhood 14:279, 1939.
245. Harper, M. H.: Celiac disease, M. J. Australia 2:540, 1930.
246. ——: Congenital steatorrhea due to pancreatic defect, Arch. Dis. Childhood 13:45, 1938.
247. Harrison, G. A.: Methods in Clinical Medicine, London, 1940.
248. Hassman, K.: The Pathogenesis of Intestinal Infantilism, Stuttgart, 1940.
249. Hay, J. D.: Folic acid in celiac disease; a study of its administration in 22 cases, Arch. Dis. Childhood 23:220, 1948.
250. Henoch, E.: Textbook of Children's Disease, ed. 10, Berlin, Hirschwald, 1899.
251. Hepler, O. E.: Manual of Clinical Laboratory Methods, ed. 4, Springfield, Ill., Thomas, 1950.
252. Hernandez Gonzales, L.: Intestinal infantilism in infant; case, Rev. med. de Canarias 1:215, 1932.
253. Herter, C.: On Infantilism from Chronic Intestinal Infection, New York, Macmillan, 1908.
254. ——: Observations on intestinal infantilism, Tr. A. Am. Physicians 25:528, 1910.
255. Hess, J. H.: Celiac disease: intestinal atrophy with dilation, chronic digestive insufficiency, chronic intestinal indigestion, intestinal infantilism (Herter), pancreatic infantilism (Bramwell), chronic fat indigestion, fat intolerance, acholia (Cheadle), Northwest Med. 25:285, 1926.
256. Hess, J. H., and Saphir, O.: Celiac disease: chronic intestinal indigestion, Am. J. Dis. Child. 48:1162, 1934.
257. Hess, J. H.: Chronic intestinal indigestion; three cases with autopsy findings, J. Pediat. 6:1, 1935.
258. Heubner, O.: Concerning severe intestinal insufficiency of children after infancy, Jahrb. f. Kinderh. 70:667, 1909.
259. Heupke, W.: Effect and use of raw foods, Medizinische Welt, 8:516, 1934.
260. Hill, E.: Chronic intestinal indigestion during the second and third years of childhood, Boston M. & S. J. 187:777, 1922.
261. Hill, E., and Bloor, W. R.: Fat excretion, J. Biol. Chem. 53:171, 1922.
262. Hodges, G. C.: Chronic intestinal indigestion, West Virginia M. J. 26:471, 1930.
263. Holmes, W. H., and Starr, P.: Nutritional disturbance in adults resembling celiac disease and sprue, J. A. M. A. 92:975, 1929.

264. Holmgren, S.: Celiac disease in uniovular twins, Nord. med. (Hygiea) **28**:2252, 1945.
265. Holt, L. E., et al.: The chemical composition of diarrheal as compared to normal stools in infants, Am. J. Dis. Child. **9**:213, 1915.
266. Holt, L. E.: Effect of cod liver oil on growth in case of intestinal infantilism, Am. J. Dis. Child. **14**:222, 1917.
267. Holt, L. E., Jr., and McIntosh, R.: Diseases of infancy and childhood, ed. 10, New York, Appleton, 1933.
268. Holt, L. E. Jr., et al.: Study of fat metabolism in infants, Acta Paediat. **26**:165, 1933.
269. Holzmann, E.: Clinical aspects and therapy of chronic digestive insufficiency in children, Münch. med. Wchnschr. **82**:864, 1935.
270. Hostomska, L.: Celiac disease in Czechoslovakia, Časop. lĕk. česk. **88**:970, 1949.
271. Hotz, H. W.: Differential diagnosis of steatorrhea, Arch. f. Verdauungskr. **63**:319, 1938.
272. Howland, J.: Prolonged intolerance to carbohydrates, Tr. Am. Pediat. Soc. **44**:11, 1921.
273. —— & Marriott, W. McK.: The indications for treatment in severe diarrhea in infancy, Arch. Pediat. **32**:374, 1915.
274. Hubbard, W. S.: The identification of emodine-bearing drugs, J. Indust. & Eng. Chem. **9**:519, 1917.
275. Huber, J., et al.: A case of infantile dystrophy, Bull. Soc. pédiat. de Paris **34**:321, 1936.
276. Huet, G. J.: Herter's disease or intestinal infantilism with chronic pulmonary infection, Maandschr. v. Kindergeneesk. **3**:345, 1934.
277. Hughes, L.: Steatorrhea, M. J. Australia **2**:671, 1939.
278. Hunter, D.: New aspects of deficiencies in nutrition, Lancet **1**:1025, 1935.
279. Hurst, A.: Pathogenesis of sprue syndrome as seen in tropical sprue, non-tropical sprue, and celiac disease. Guy's Hosp. Rep. **91**:1, 1942.
280. Husler, I.: Chronic intestinal insufficiency, Münch. Ges. f. Kinderh. **28**:190, 1924.
281. Hutchinson, R.: Celiac disease, Practitioner **87**:147, 1911.
282. ——: A clinical lecture on celiac disease, Brit. J. Child. Dis. **9**:229, 1912.
283. Irish, H. E.: Banana therapy in celiac disease, Am. J. Dis. Child. **31**:303, 1926.
284. ——: Case of celiac disease with banana treatment, Arch. Pediat. **43**:533, 1926.
285. Israels, M. C. G., and Sharp, J.: Idiopathic steatorrhea (non-tropical sprue) with megaloblastic anemia, Lancet **1**:752, 1950.

286. Ivy, A. C.: Certain aspects of the applied physiology of external pancreatic secretion, Am. J. Digest. Dis. & Nutrition 3:677, 1936.
287. Janssen, E.: Intestinal infantilism in children and sprue in adults, Geneesk. tijdschr. v. Nederl.-Indie 77:2552, 1937.
288. Jennings, K.: Recent advances in celiac disease, M. Times New York 74:99, 1946.
289. Johnson, F. E.: Chronic intestinal indigestion in children, New York State J. M. 23:192, 1923.
290. Johnson, K.: Intestinal infantilism with severe anemia treated with parenteral administration of vitamin B; two cases, Nord. med. (Norsk, mag. f. laegevidensk.) 13:165, 1942.
291. Johnston, J. A.: Place of the banana in the diet of children, J. Am. Dietet. A. 3:93, 1927.
292. Johnston, J. A., and Howard, P. J.: Celiac syndrome; factors influencing its development with particular reference to hypothyroidism as contributing cause, J. Pediat. 35:1, 1949.
293. Josephs, H. W.: Studies in vitamin A; relation of vitamin A and carotene to serum lipoids, Bull. Johns Hopkins Hosp. 65:112, 1939.
294. Jungdell, I.: Case of intestinal infantilism with osteopathia, Acta paediat. 14:259, 1932.
295. Justin-Besancon, L., et al.: Nicotinic acid in idiopathic steatorrhea: biologic and nosologic observations, Bull. et mém. Soc. méd. d. hôp. de Paris 55:1141, 1939.
296. Kahn, B. S.: The effect of banana powder feeding on the fecal flora of infants, Arch. Pediat. 50:330, 1933.
297. Kantor, J. L.: Synopsis of Digestive Diseases, St. Louis, Mosby, 1937.
298. ——: Roentgen diagnosis of idiopathic steatorrhea and allied conditions: practical value of "moulage sign," Am. J. Roentgenol. 41:758, 1939.
299. Kark, R., et al.: Hemorrhagic diathesis in idiopathic steatorrhea, Quart. J. Med. 9:247, 1940.
300. Karlen, K. H.: Idiopathic steatorrhea, Nord. med. 43:737, 1950.
301. ——: Non-tropical sprue: case, Nord. med. 43:759, 1950.
302. Karrer, P.: Organic Chemistry, ed. 2 in Eng., New York, Elsevier, 1946.
303. Keele, K. D.: Celiac disease showing unusual features, Proc. Roy. Soc. Med. London, 28:663, 1934-1935.
304. Kehrer, E.: Tetany and osteomalacia, probably on basis of celiac disease, with symptoms of pluriglandular insufficiency, Ztschr. f. Geburtsk. u. Gynäk. 116:141, 1938.

305. Kellett, C. E.: Method of estimating fat absorption, Lancet 2:1270, 1932.
306. Kellie, K.: Two cases of infantilism, Proc. Roy. Soc. Med. Child. Sect. 4:59, 1910-1911.
307. Kendall, A. I.: Bacillus infantilis and its relations to infantilism, J. Biol. Chem. 5:419, 1909.
308. Kerley, C. G.: Further contribution, Arch. Pediat. 47:24, 1930.
309. ——: Therapy without use of cow's milk, Arch. Pediat. 48:393, 1930.
310. Kerley, C. A., and Craig, H. R.: Observations on celiac disease, Am. J. Dis. Child. 28:520, 1924.
311. Kerley, C. A.: Celiac disease, Internat. Clin. 3:268, 1924.
312. Khourine, Y.: Digestion of cellulose by human intestinal flora, Ann. de l' Institut Pasteur 37:711, 1928.
313. Kleinschmidt, H.: Chronic diarrhea in children, Jahresk. f. Aerztl. Fortbild. 13:16, 1922.
314. ——: Raw fruit in intestinal infantilism, Jahresk. f. ärtzl. Fortbild. 22:12, 1931.
315. ——: Diseases of the stomach and intestines, in Pfaundler's "The Diseases of Children," Philadelphia, Lippincott, 1935.
316. Knauer, H.: The question of the blood-sugar curve, Monatschr. f. kinderh. 64:356, 1936.
317. Knopfelmacher, W.: Herter's infantilism, Wien. med. Wchnschr. 76:1348, 1926.
318. Konstam, G.: Idiopathic steatorrhea with osteoporosis, tetany, and megalocytic anemia, Proc. Roy. Soc. Med. 29:629, 1936.
319. Konstam, G., and Gordon, H.: Idiopathic steatorrhea with skin lesions and megalocytic anemia, Proc. Roy. Soc. Med. 29:629, 1936.
320. Kramer, B.: Celiac disease, Rev. Gastroenterol. 11:256, 1944.
321. Krarup, M. B., and Gørtz, S.: Genesis of low dextrose tolerance curve in idiopathic steatorrhea, Bibliot. f. laeger. 128:352, 1936.
322. Kuhlmann, F.: Intestinal findings, Monatschr. f. Kinderh. 73:367, 1938.
323. Kundratitz, K.: Case of Herter's infantilism, Mitt. des Ges. f. inn. Med. u. Kinderh. Wien 24:7, 1925.
324. ——: Pathogenesis of intestinal infantilism, Jahrb. f. Kinderh. 116:310, 1927.
325. Kunstadter, R. H.: Gastro-intestinal allergy and the celiac syndrome, J. Pediat. 21:193, 1942.
326. Ladd, M.: Digestive disorders in children, J. S. Carolina M. A. 12:141, 1916.

327. Lages Netto, J.: Intestinal infantilism or celiac disease, Pediat. prat. S. Paolo 4:401, 1932-1933.
328. Lahdensu, S., and Somersalo, O.: Celiac disease in uniovular twins: case, Nord. med. 32:2819, 1946.
329. Landau, G.: Case of celiac disease, Warsz. czas. lek. 14:465, 1937.
330. Lane, D. E.: Nutritive and therapeutic value of the banana, Am. J. Phys. Ther. 11:14, 1934.
331. Lange, O.: Concerning chronic intestinal insufficiency of children, Nederl. tijdschr. v. geneesk. 2:289, 1910.
332. Langstein, L.: Intestinal infantilism, Med. germano-hispano-americana 1:29, 1925.
333. Lapin, J. H.: Recurrent and chronic diarrhea in infancy and childhood, Am. J. Dis. Child. 67:139, 1944.
334. Laszt, L., and Verzar, F.: Concerning chronic iodic-acid poisoning and its significance in Gee-Herter's disease, Pflüger's Arch. 237:483, 1936.
335. Laurie, W. S.: Celiac disease, M. J. Australia 1:109, 1924.
336. Lawaetz, B., and Vogtmøller, P.: Fat metabolism: applicability of hemolipocrit method and physiology and pathology of hyperlipemia in different diseases particularly idiopathic steatorrhea (sprue, non-tropical sprue, intestinal infantilism), Hospitalstid. 79:1009, 1936.
337. Leedham-Green, J.: Bananas, Middlesex Hosp. J. 30:49, 1930.
338. Lehmann, F.: Bone changes with intestinal infantilism, Monatschr. f. Kinderh. 30:124, 1925.
339. Lehndorff, H., and Mautner, H.: Herter's and Heubner's syndromes, Ergeb. d. inn. med. u. Kinderh. 31:456, 1927.
340. Lesne, E., and Launay, C.: Case with nanism and osteoporosis: recovery from intestinal syndrome: persistence of osteoporosis: role of C avitaminosis, Bull. et mém. Soc. méd. d. hôp. de Paris 54:851, 1938.
341. Levent, R.: Celiac disease, Gas. d. hôp. civ. et mil. 97:1093, 1924.
342. Levinsohn, S. A.: Summary of present conceptions, Arch. Pediat. 44:368, 1927.
343. Levy, G., and Lander, E.: Clinical study of intestinal infantilism: four cases, Arch. de méd. d. enfan. 40:207, 1937.
344. Lewes, D.: Modern treatment and management, M. Presse 217:65, 1947.
345. Lewis, H. B., and Lough, S. A.: A metabolic study of a case of cystinuria, J. Biol. Chem. 45:81, 1929.
346. Lewy, F. H.: The physiologic action of the vitamin B. complex, Phila. Confinia Neurologica, 3:74, 1940.
347. Lichtenstein, A.: Toward knowledge of so-called intestinal infantilism (Heubner's chronic intestinal insufficiency), Acta paediat. 1:105, 1921.

348. Little, H.: Chronic intestinal indigestion, Canad. M. A. J. 20:500, 1929.

349. Lodi, G.: Therapy of celiac disease, Med. inf. Roma 7:325, 1936.

350. Loeschke, A.: Concerning the incidence and the significance of disorders of internal secretion in celiac disease, Monatschr. f. Kinderh. 70:86, 1937.

351. Lous, P.: Differential diagnosis of steatorrhea, Ugesk. f. laeger. 106:519, 1944.

352. Lups, S.: Muscular dystrophy in steatorrhea, Acta med. Scandinav. 106:557, 1941.

353. Luzzatti, L., and Hansen, A. E.: Serum lipids in celiac syndrome (on basis of cystic fibrosis of the pancreas), J. Pediat. 24:417, 1944.

354. MacCrudden, F. H.: Chemical studies of intestinal infantilism: endogenous metabolism: kreatinin, kreatin, uric acid, J. Exper. Med. 15:107, 1912.

355. MacCrudden, F. H., and Fales, H. L.: Complete balance studies on nitrogen, sulphur, phosphorus, calcium, and magnesium in intestinal infantilism, J. Exper. Med. 15:450, 1912.

356. MacCrudden, F. H.: The nature and origin of the nitrogen in the feces in infantilism, J. Exper. Med. 17:20, 1913.

357. ——: The cause of the excessive calcium excretion through the feces in infantilism, J. Exper. Med. 17:169, 1913.

358. ——: Intestinal absorption in infantilism, J. Exper. Med. 17:199, 1913.

359. ——: The cause of failure to develop in infantilism, J. Exper. Med. 17:202, 1913.

360. MacLean, A. B., and Sullivan, R. C.: Carbohydrate tolerance in infants and young children, Am. J. Dis. Child. 38:16, 1929.

361. Mach, R. S.: Cured case of Gee-Herter's disease in man, Arch. d. mal. de l'app. digestif 26:544, 1936.

362. Macrae, O., and Morris, N.: Metabolism studies, Arch. Dis. Childhood, 6:75, 1931.

363. Mader, A.: Idiopathic intestinal insufficiency: a characteristic disease of childhood, Deutsch. med. Wchnschr. 50:604, 1924.

364. ——: Etiology and treatment of idiopathic digestive insufficiency, Klin. Wchnschr. 5:367, 1926.

365. Magni, L., and Pirami, A.: A case of celiac disease of pancreatic origin, Riv. di clin. pediat. 24:145, 1926.

366. Maldague, L.: Intestinal infantilism, Rev. med. Louvain 14:217, 1939.

367. Mann, F. C.: Modified physiologic processes following total removal of liver, J. A. M. A. 85:1472, 1925.

368. Marfan, A. B.: Celiac disease, Nourrisson 17:321, 1929.
369. ——: Celiac disease, Nourrisson 22:384, 1934.
370. Marriott, W. McK.: Chronic digestive insufficiency (celiac disease) M. Clin. N. America 6:91, 1922.
371. May, A.: Cases of acholia in children, Med. Mag. London 1905.
372. May, C. D., and McCreary, J. F.: Glucose tolerance test: significance of low blood-sugar curves, J. Pediat. 17:143, 1940.
373. May, C. D.: The absorption of vitamin A in celiac disease. J. Pediat. 18:200, 1941.
374. May, C. D., et al: Treatment of patients with fibrosis of the pancreas, Am. J. Dis. Child. 75:470, 1948.
375. May, C. D., et al: Cause of celiac disease, J. Pediat. 21:289, 1942.
376. May, W. J.: Celiac disease, J. Bowman Gray School Med. 2:64, 1944.
377. Mayerhofer, E.: Advantages and disadvantages of use of garlic in children, Arch. f. Kinderh. 102:106, 1934.
378. McCarrison, R.: Influence of deficiency of accessory food-factors on the intestines, Brit. J. Med. 2:36, 1919.
379. McKhann, C. F., et al.: An association of gastro-intestinal allergy with the celiac syndrome, J. Pediat. 22:362, 1943.
380. McLean, A. B., and Sullivan, R. C.: Carbohydrate tolerance in infants and young children, Am. J. Dis. Child. 38:16, 1929.
381. Mendel, L. B.: Nutrition, the Chemistry of Life, New Haven, Yale, 1923.
382. Meneghello, J., and Andurraga, O.: Report of case observed three years, Rev. chilena de pediat. 17:325, 1946.
383. Merilini, F.: A case of infantile dystrophy, Osp. psichiat. nat. 3:350, 1935.
384. Meyer, A.: Diagnosis and therapy, Ztschr. f. klin. Med. 119:667, 1932.
385. Michelmore, R. G.: Ultra-violet radiation in celiac disease, Lancet. 2:1264, 1926.
386. Mikulowski, W.: Gee's disease, Polska gaz. lĕuk. 9:137, 1930.
387. ——: Gee's disease: case, Arch. de méd. d. enf. 33:416, 1930.
388. ——: Case of celiac disease, Acta paediat. 10:592, 1931.
389. Miller, R.: Celiac disease, Lancet. 199:1166, 1920.
390. ——: Fatal case of celiac infantilism with comments on morbid anatomy of celiac disease, Lancet. 1:743, 1921.
391. ——: Celiac and allied types of infantilism, a retrospect and bibliography, Brit. J. Child. Dis. 18:11, 1921.
392. ——: Two cases of celiac infantilism in the convalescent (non-diarrheic) stage, Proc. Roy. Soc. Med. London, 16:22, 1922-1923.

393. ——: On the treatment of celiac disease, Arch. Pediat. 11:88, 1923.
394. ——: Pathogenesis of celiac disease, Arch. Pediat. 40:88, 1923.
395. ——: Case of celiac disease showing symptoms of megalocolon, with autopsy, Brit. J. Child. Dis. 20:88, 1923.
396. ——:Treatment of celiac disease, Lancet. 2:1099, 1923.
397. ——: Celiac disease: its definition and diagnosis, Lancet. 1:330, 1926.
398. ——:Gluteal wasting as sign of celiac disease, Arch. Dis. childhood. 2:189, 1927.
399. ——: Celiac disease, in Brit. Encyclopaedia of Medical Practice, London, 1937.
400. Miller, R., and Perkins, H.: Congenital steatorrhea, Quart. J. Med. 14:1, 1920.
401. Miller, R.: Non-diarrheic type of celiac disease; form of chronic fat indigestion in children, Lancet. 1:72, 1923.
402. Miller, R., et al.: Celiac infantilism: its fat digestion and treatment by bile salts, Lancet 199:894, 1910.
403. Miller, R., et al.: Celiac infantilism: its fat digestion and treatment by bile salts, Lancet 2:894, 1920.
404. Mindline, J., and Rosenheim, M. L.: Duodeno-colic fistula simulating idiopathic steatorrhea, Lancet 2:764, 1935.
405. Mitchell, A. G. and Nelson, W. E.: Textbook of Pediatrics, ed. 4, Philadelphia, Saunders, 1945.
406. Mogensen, E.: Idiopathic steatorrhea; three cases, Hospitalstid. 79:1032, 1936.
407. ——: Idiopathic steatorrhea: three cases, Quart. J. Med. 6:119, 1937.
408. Mohamed, H.: Contribution to a Study of Celiac Disease or Intestinal Infantilism, Lausanne, 1934.
409. Møller, P. F., et al.: Roentgenological investigation of the small intestine in celiac disease, Acta Paediat. 35:233, 1948 (Supp. I).
410. Molnar, S., and Noszko, S.: Concerning carbohydrate metabolism in nervous disorders caused by vitamin B1, Klin. Wchnschr. Budapest, 17:938, 1938.
411. Mondolfo, E.: Case of celiac disease, Policlinico. 43:237, 1936.
412. Moore, C.: Disturbance in growth, M. Clin. North America. 12:433, 1928.
413. Moore, F.: Celiac disease, J. Iowa M. Soc. 16:273, 1926.
414. Moore, H., et al.: Gee's disease, Lancet. 2:1167, 1934.
415. Moore, H.: Gee-Thaysen's disease; idiopathic steatorrhea of adults and adolescents in non-tropical countries, Quart. J. Med. 5:481, 1936.
416. Moorhead, P. G.: Pancreatic and intestinal infantilism, Dublin J. M. Sci. 149:1, 1920.

417. Morano Brandi, J. F.: Celiac disease and Verzar theory of pathogenesis: case, Rev. med. la Plata 3:27, 1945.
418. Morse, J. L.: Celiac disease, New Eng. J. Med. 204:662, 1931.
419. Morse, J. L., and Talbot, F. B.: Diseases of Nutrition and Infant Feeding, New York, Macmillan, 1915.
420. Mouriquand, G., et al.: Bioclinical study of enteropathies due to deficiencies, with special reference to vitamin C, Presse méd. 47:1229, 1939.
421. Muggia, A.: Influence of fat in milk on physical development of infant: case of celiac disease, Lattante 6:503, 1935.
422. Mumford, W.: Arrested growth and chronic diarrhea, Manchester Med. Chron. 15:169, 1908.
423. Muncrieff, A., and Payne, W. W.: Etiology; preliminary commmunication on blood fat, Arch. Dis. Childhood 3:257, 1928.
424. Munilla, A.: Celiac disease and modern concepts of intestinal absorption, Pediat. americas 1:549, 1943.
425. Murphy, G.: Non-tropical sprue, Rev. med. argent. 64:679, 1950.
426. Neale, A. V.: Prognosis and treatment, Birmingham Med. Rev. 5:77, 1930.
427. ——: Prognosis and treatment, Clin. J. 59:313, 1930.
428. Neale, A. V., et al.: Prognosis of celiac disease with comments on hematologic characteristics, Am. J. Dis. Child. 50:1502, 1935.
429. Neff, F. C.: Recent advances in the treatment of celiac disease, Quart. Bull. Kansas City Clin. Soc. 2:9, 1925-1926.
430. Nelson, M. V.: Metabolic observations on four cases, Am. J. Dis. Child. 39:76, 1930.
431. Newsome, J.: Secretin test of pancreatic function: use in steatorrhea, Gastroenterologia, 74:257, 1948-1949.
432. Nihar, K. N.: A case of celiac disease, Indian Med. Gaz. 74:96, 1939.
433. Nobel, E.: A case of intestinal infantilism (Herter), Mitt. d. Ges. f. inn. Med. u. Kinderh. 12:115, 1913.
434. Nyman, E.: Ulcerous jejunoileitis with symptomatic sprue, Acta med. scandinav. 134:275, 1949.
435. Odegaard, A.: Resorption research on celiac disease, Acta paediat. 35:235, 1948 (Supp. I).
436. Ogilvie, J. W.: Gastric secretion, Arch. Dis. Childhood 10:93, 1935.
437. Oliaro, G.: History and general review, Minerva med. 8:21, 1928.
438. Opie, E. A.: The nursing of celiac disease, Nurs. Times London 32:106, 1936.

439. Orgel, S. Z.: A case of intestinal intoxication (Herter's intestinal infantilism), Med. Rec. 99:269, 1921.
440. Ostheimer, M.: Infantilism of Herter, Brit. J. Child. Dis. 9:460, 1912.
441. O'Sullivan, J. F., and Moore, H.: Gee-Thaysen's disease (idiopathic steatorrhea of adults and adolescents in nontropical countries), with note on postscriptum, Brit. M. J. 1:183, 1941.
442. Parmalee, A. H.: Pathology of steatorrhea, Am. J. Dis. Child. 50:1418, 1935.
443. Parsons, L. G.: Bone changes occurring in renal and celiac infantilism and their relationship to rickets: celiac rickets, Arch. Dis. Childhood 2:198, 1927.
444. —: Recent advances in our knowledge; Ingleby lectures, Lancet 2:485, 1928.
445. —: Fat metabolism, Acta paediat. 11:156, 1930.
446. —: Celiac disease, Lancet 1:61, 1931.
447. —: Rachford memorial lectures, Am. J. Dis. Child. 43:1293, 1932.
448. —: Nutritional problems of childhood (Dawson Williams memorial lecture), Brit. M. J. 2:929, 1938.
449. Parsons, L. G., and Hawksley, J. C.: Anemias of prematurity, scurvy, and celiac disease in infancy and early childhood, Arch. Dis. Childhood 8:117, 1933.
450. Passini, F.: Pancreatic disorder as cause of lack of development, Deutsch. med. Wchnschr. 31:851, 1919.
451. Paterson, D., et al.: Vitamin B complex and concentrated liver, Arch. Dis. Childhood 19:99, 1944.
452. Payne, G. W.: Celiac disease, Kentucky M. J. 25:373, 1927.
453. Pease, M. C., and Rose, A. R.: Banana as a food for children, Am. J. Dis. Child. 14:379, 1917.
454. Pedvis, S.: Fat absorption, McGill M. J. 12:249, 1943.
455. Petuely, F., and Kristen, G.: Investigation of the conversion of the intestinal flora of the infant, Ann. paediat. 172:183, 1949.
456. Philipsborn, H. F., et al.: The diagnosis of fibrocystic disease of the pancreas, J. Pediat. 25:284, 1944.
457. Philipsborn, H. F.: Analysis of duodenal drainage in steatorrhea (differential diagnosis of fibrocystic disease of pancreas and celiac disease), J. Pediat. 26:107, 1945.
458. Pipping, W.: Celiac disease, Finska läk.-sälisk. handl. 65:491, 1923.
459. —: Celiac disease, Acta paediat. 3:342, 1924.
460. Pivani, A.: Fanconi method (vegetables and raw fruit), Pediatria d. med. prat. 7:257, 1932.
461. Podolsky, E.: Fruits and health, New Health 11:12, 1936.
462. Ponticaccia, M.: Celiac disease, Med. inf. Roma 8:15, 1937.

463. Porter, L., and Hunter, C.: Some studies on sugar in infant feeding, Am. J. Dis. Child. 10:77, 1915.
464. Porter, L., et al.: Certain nutritional disorders of children associated with a putrefactive intestinal flora, Am. J. Dis. Child. 18:254, 1919.
465. Poynton, F. J., and Cole, L. B.: Case of celiac disease with glycosuria, Brit. J. Child. Dis. 22:30, 1925.
466. Poynton, F. J., and Patterson: The occurrence of ascites of a non-tuberculous origin in chronic recurrent diarrhea in childhood, Lancet, 186:1588, 1914.
467. Poynton, F. J.: A fatal case of celiac disease infantilism, Lancet 200:826, 1921.
468. Poynton, F. J., et al.: A contribution to the study of a group of cases of chronic recurrent diarrhea in childhood, Proc. Roy. Soc. Med. 7:10, 1913-1914.
469. Pratt, E. L., and Fahey, K. R.: Clinical adequacy of single measurement of vitamin A absorption, Am. J. Dis. Child. 63:83, 1944.
470. Priesel, R.: Intestinal infantilism, Wien. klin. Wchnschr. 46:947, 1933.
471. Pritchard, E.: New method (of treatment), Practitioner 133:597, 1934.
472. Radl, R. B., and Fallon, M.: Non-tropical sprue with duodenal involvement and tetany, Arch. Int. Med. 50:595, 1932.
473. Raistrick, H., et al.: Emodine monomethyl ether from aspergillus glaucus link grown on glucose, J. Chem. Soc. 1:80, 1937.
474. Rascovsky, A.: Herter's intestinal infantilism or Heubner's chronic digestive insufficiency in older children; case, Arch. argent. de pediat. 7:25, 1931.
475. Rauch, S., et al.: Congenital familial steatorrhea with fibromatosis of pancreas and bronchiolectasis, J. Pediat. 14:462, 1939.
476. Recalde Questas, J. C., and Travella, E. A.: Concerning celiac disease, Actas congr. nac. med. Rosario 5:1187, 1934.
477. Reiche, E.: Case of chronic intestinal insufficiency, Ges. f. inn. Med. u. Kinderh. Berlin 11:11, 1912.
478. Remington, J. P.: Practice of Pharmacy, ed. 9, Easton, Pa., Mack, 1948.
479. Rentoul, J. L.: Pancreatic infantilism, Brit. M. J. 2:1695, 1904.
480. Rettger, L. F., and Cheplin, H. A.: A Treatise on the Transformation of the Intestinal Flora, New Haven, Yale, 1921.
481. Reuben, M. S.: Celiac disease, Arch. Pediat. 45:498, 1928.

482. Reyher, P.: The question of chronic intestinal insufficiency (intestinal infantilism), Arch. f. Kinderh. 75:72, 1925.
483. Rice, C. V.: Treatment from standpoint of vitamin deficiency, Arch. Pediat. 47:572, 1930.
484. ——: Therapy from standpoint of vitamin deficiency, Arch. Pediat. 50:358, 1933.
485. ——: Success of treating from standpoint of vitamin deficiency, Arch. Pediat. 53:626, 1936.
486. Rice, M. E.: Physiologic interpretation of clinical changes, J. Bauman Gray School Med. 1:144, 1943.
487. Riddell, W. J.: Celiac disease associated with night blindness and xerosis conjunctivae, Tr. Ophth. Soc. U. K. 53:295, 1933.
488. Riesel, Z.: Concerning intestinal infantilism, Deutsch. med. Wchnschr. 38:1720, 1912.
489. Rietschel, H.: Pathogenesis of sprue or celiac disease in children, Schweiz. med. Wchnschr. 67:983, 1937.
490. ——: Role of vitamin B complex in celiac disease, Verhandl. d. deutsch. Ges. f. inn. Med. Cong. 50:397, 1938.
491. ——: Pathogenesis of sprue or celiac disease in children, Deutsch. med. Wchnschr. 64:73, 1938.
492. Riley, I. D.: Metabolic eczema in idiopathic steatorrhea, Lancet 1:262, 1939.
493. Rinkel, H. J.: Food allergy, J. Pediat. 32:266, 1948.
494. Robalinho Cavalcanti, J., and Villaca, M.: Celiac disease, Brasil. med. 52:358, 1938.
495. Roberts, C. G.: Therapy in adults with sugarless milk, bananas, and meat, Lancet 1:130, 1934.
496. Rogers, L.: Sprue and celiac disease, Brit. M. J. 2:1720, 1923.
497. Rogers, L., et al.: Discussion on sprue and celiac disease, Proc. Roy. Soc. Med. 17:11, 1924.
498. Rohmer, P.: Celiac disease, Le concours medicale 49:6, 1927.
499. ——: Celiac disease, Strasbourg med. 85:351, 1927.
500. ——: The stimulating action of vitamin C in certain forms of chronic indigestion in infants, Bull. Soc. de pédiat. de Paris 27:279, 1929.
501. ——: Relation of chronic dyspepsia in children after first years to celiac disease, Bull. Soc. de pédiat. de Paris 29:347, 1931.
502. ——: Celiac disease, in Traité de médecine des enfants, Paris, Masson, 1934.
503. Rony, H. R., and Ching, T. T.: Studies on fat metabolism; the effect of certain hormones on fat transport, Endocrinology 14:355, 1950.
504. Ross, C. W.: Intestinal absorption with some remarks on effect of liver extract upon carbohydrate metabolism, Tr. Roy. Soc. Trop. Med. & Hyg. 30:33, 1936.

505. ——: Impaired glucose tolerance in certain alimentary disorders of childhood, with remarks on their treatment with liver extract, Lancet, 2:556, 1936.
506. Rossi, R.: Case of celiac disease, Rev. Asoc. méd. argent. 48:39, 1934.
507. ——: Case; possible etiology, Arch. de med. int. 1:288, 1935.
508. Rossi, R., and Lozana, F.: Possible etiology; presence of monilia albicans in case, An. fac. de cien. med. de La Plata 1:133, 1937.
509. Rossi, V., and Sanna, G.: Case of celiac disease, Riv. di clin. pediat. 29:874, 1931.
510. Roviralta Astoul, E.: Surgical therapy; preliminary report, Rev. espan. pediat. 3:194, 1947.
511. Rüggesborg, M. M.: Concerning Schütz-Heubner-Herter's Disease, Dissertation, Cologne, 1926.
512. Rurah, J.: Samuel Gee, Am. J. Dis. Child. 48:159, 1934.
513. Ryle, J. A.: Celiac disease, Lancet 204:206, 1923.
514. ——:Etiology, fatty stools from obstruction of lacteals, with note on celiac affection, Guy's Hosp. Rep. 74:1, 1924.
515. Sabri, I. A., et al.: Celiac disease in Egypt, J. Egypt. M. A. 17:930, 1934.
516. Salmi, T.: Heubner-Herter's disease, Duodecim 52:1038, 1936.
517. Santana y Gonzales, R.: Celiac syndrome; study apropos of clinical case, Rev. cubana pediat. 18:266, 1946.
518. Sarachaga, F.: Intestinal infantilism, Progressos de la clin. 40:526, 1932.
519. ——: Case of celiac disease, An. casa de salud Valdecilla 3:202, 1932.
520. Sarma, A. V. S.: Celiac disease, antiseptic 41:311, 1944.
521. Sauer, L. W.: Diet in celiac disease (chronic intestinal indigestion) : simple three phase high protein diet, Am. J. Dis. Child. 29:155, 1925.
522. ——: Etiology, prognosis, and standardization of treatment, Am. J. Dis. Child. 34:934, 1927.
523. Sauer, L. W., Schick, B., and Haas, S. V.: Discussion of celiac disease, Central States Pediat. Soc. 3rd Session, 1925.
524. Savage, J.: Celiac disease, Colorado Med. 21:136, 1924.
525. Saxl, N. T.: Celiac disease, M. Rec. 143:110, 1936.
526. ——: Pediatric Dietetics, Philadelphia, 1937.
527. Schaap, L.: Intestinal infantilism, Arch. d. mal. de l'app. digestif. 16:914, 1926.
528. Schalij, F. A.: Intestinal infantilism, Geneesk. gid. 2:1157; 1181, 1927.
529. Schachter, M.: Behavior of children with Herter-Heubner's disease, Clin. pediat. 15:747, 1933.

530. ——: Future of children having celiac disease, Progrès méd. 2:1187, 1934.
531. ——: Celiac disease, Rev. méd. de Nancy 65:860, 1937.
532. Schick, B., and Wagner, R.: Concerning intestinal insufficiency in childhood (atrophia pluriglandularis digestiva), Ztschr. f. Kinderh. 35:263, 1923.
533. Schiff, E.: Celiac Disease, Berlin and Vienna, Urban, 1934.
534. Schiff, E., and Kochman, R.: The pathogenesis of digestive disorders in infants, Jahrb. f. Kinderh. 99:181, 1942.
535. Schlesinger, B., and Keele, K. D.: Case showing unusual features successfully treated with insulin and glucose, Arch. Dis. Childhood 10:149, 1935.
536. Schmidt, A., and Strasburger, J.: The Human Feces in Normal and Pathological Circumstances with Special Reference to Clinical Examination, Berlin, Hirschwald, 1910.
537. Schutz, R.: Putrefactive bacteria as a cause of chronic digestive disturbances, Deutsch. Arch. f. klin. Med. 80:580, 1904.
538. ——: Chronic stomach-intestine dyspepsia in childhood, Jahrb. f. Kinderh. 62:794, 1905.
539. ——: Concerning chronic stomach-intestine dyspepsia diarrhea of childhood, Therapeut. Montschr. 23:354, 1909.
540. ——: Chronic stomach-intestine dyspepsia of childhood: so-called Herter-Heubner syndrome; Heubner's intestinal insufficiency of childhood, Berl. klin. Wchnschr. 50:2018, 1913.
541. Schwachman, H., et al.: Pancreatic function and disease in early life, Am. J. Dis. Child. 66:418, 1943.
542. Schwarz-Thiene, E.: Corticoadrenal insufficiency in celiac disease, Minerva pediat. 2:149, 1950.
543. Schweizer, F., and Guridi, C. I.: A case of celiac disease, Arch. argent. pediat. 6:371, 1935.
544. Scolari, E.: Chronic idiopathic steatosis following gastroenterostomy, Minerva med. 1:305, 1945.
545. Scott, G. E. M.: Survey from Children's Hospital, Melbourne, M. J. Australia 1:659, 1946.
546. ——: Celiac disease and celiac syndrome, M. J. Australia 1:37, 1950.
547. Scott, J. P.: Intestinal infantilism with report of case, Arch. Pediat. 45:604, 1928.
548. Segall, D.: Contribution to clinical studies on celiac disease, Rev. st. med. Bucarest 22:812, 1933.
549. Sheldon, W.: Relation between dietary starch and fat absorption, Arch. Dis. Childhood 28:41, 1949.
550. Sheldon, W., and MacMahon, A.: Studies in celiac disease: fat absorption, Arch. Dis. Childhood 24:245, 1949.

551. Sherman, DeW. H., and Lohnes, H. R.: The effects of sugars on the gastric secretions of infants, Arch. Pediat. 31:749, 1914.
552. Shippman, F.: Celiac disease, Canad. M. A. J. 34:243, 1936.
553. Shohl, A. T., et al.: Studies of nitrogen and fat metabolism on infants and children with pancreatic fibrosis, J. Pediat. 23:267, 1943.
554. Silverman, A. C.: Celiac disease, New York State J. Med. 32:1055, 1932.
555. Small, A. M.: Non-tropical sprue: clinical observations, South. M. J. 28:516, 1935.
556. Small, A. M., et al.: Non-tropical sprue (chronic idiopathic steatorrhea), Proc. Staff Meet. Mayo Clin. 10:177, 1935.
557. Smallwood, W. C., and Shippam, F.: Prognosis of celiac disease with comment on hematologic characteristics, Am. J. Dis. Child. 50:1502, 1935.
558. Smith, F. R.: Complicated by purpura, Boston M. & S. J. 197:658, 1927.
559. Smith-Siversten, C.: Two cases of intestinal infantilism with remarks on nature of this disease, Med. rev. Bergen 47:16, 1930.
560. Snell, A. M.: Clinical observations on non-tropical sprue, Arch. Int. Med. 57:837, 1936.
561. Snell, A. M., et al.: Non-tropical sprue, Proc. Staff Meet. Mayo Clin. 10:177, 1935.
562. Snell, A. M., and Camp, J. D.: Chronic idiopathic steatorrhea; roentgenographic observation, Arch. Int. Med. 53:615, 1934.
563. Sollmann, T.: A Manual of Pharmacology, ed. 7, Philadelphia, Saunders, 1948.
564. Somersalo, O.: Necessity for examination of duodenal fluid, Nord. med. 32:2779, 1946.
565. ——: Intravenous glucose tolerance tests relating to patients suffering from celiac disease, Acta paediat. 35:234, 1948.
566. ——: Staub-Traugott effect in healthy children and in children with celiac disease, Acta paediat. 38:579, 1949.
567. Southworth, T. S.: The influence of starch on infant digestion, Am. J. Obst. 70:520, 1914.
568. Sperry, W. M., and Bloor, W. R.: Fat excretion; quantitative relations of fecal lipoids, J. Biol. Chem. 60:26, 1924.
569. Stalder, H.: Effects of desoxycorticosterone acetate (adrenal preparation) on idiopathic steatorrhea, Gastroenterologia 65:280, 1940.
570. Stannus, H. S.: Sprue, Tr. Roy. Soc. Trop. Med. & Hyg. 36:123, 1942.
571. Stearns, G., et al.: Diet in malnutrition and celiac disease with special reference to use of dextrose and bananas, J. Pediat. 18:12, 1941.

572. Steen, R. E.: Celiac disease, Brit. J. Child. Dis. 30:163, 1933.
573. Stegen, G.: Celiac syndrome, Rev. chilena pediat. 18:761, 1947.
574. Stheeman, H. A.: Ventraemon (desiccated stomach preparation) in intestinal infantilism, Nederl. tijdschr. v. geneesk. 76:4823, 1932.
575. Still, G. F.: Celiac disease, Lancet 2:163; 227, 1918.
576. Stolte, K.: Severe diarrhea in neuropathological children, Jahrb. f. Kinderh. 86:89, 1917.
577. Stoos, P.: Concerning Herter's intestinal infantilism on the basis of fourteen observed cases, Cor.-bl. f. schweiz. Aertzte, Basel 47:1734, 1917.
578. ——: Intestinal infantilism, Rev. méd. de la Suisse Normande 37:582, 1917.
579. Storts, B. P.: Two cases of celiac disease, Southwest Med. 18:302, 1934.
580. Strandqvist, B.: Severe anemia and hemorrhagic diathesis in Herter-Heubner's disease, Rev. frse. de pediat. 5:728, 1929.
581. Stransky, E.: Intestinal infantilism: celiac disease: and Herter-Heubner's disease, Rev. frse. de pediat. 5:587, 1929.
582. Stross, J.: Treatment with banana; case, Wien. med. Wchnschr. 78:818, 1928.
583. Suarez Perdigero, M.: Celiac disease and celiac syndrome: concept and pathogenesis, Rev. espan. pediat. 1:683, 1945.
584. Suranyi, G.: Celiac disease, Orv. hetil. 79:201, 1935.
585. Svensgaard, E.: Blood sugar in intestinal infantilism, Acta paediat. 46:467, 1929.
586. ——: Blood sugar, Acta paediat. 12:1, 1931.
587. Sylvester, P. H. and Hibben, F. H.: The relation of the gas bacillus to infectious diarrhea and other digestive disturbances in children, Arch. Pediat. 32:457, 1915.
588. Tauw, J. F.: Liver extract in steatorrhea, Nederl. tijdschr. v. geneesk. 78:5210, 1934.
589. Taylor, R.: Celiac disease, Arch. Pediat. 39:376, 1922.
590. ——: Celiac disease, Am. J. Dis. Child. 25:46, 1923.
591. Telfer, S. V.: Mineral metabolism, Glasgow M. J. 109:306, 1928.
592. Tepley, L. J., et al.: The intestinal synthesis of niacin and folic acid in the rat, Am. J. Psysiol. 148:91, 1947.
593. Teyschl, O.: Herter's intestinal infantilism, Časop. lěk. česk. 69:1558, 1930.
594. Thaysen, T. E. H.: Celiac affection; idiopathic steatorrhea, Lancet 1:1086, 1929.
595. ——: Blood sugar regulation in idiopathic steatorrhea; origin of low blood sugar curve, Arch. Int. Med. 44:477, 1929.

596. ——: Celiac disease, Hospitalstid. 74:601, 1931.
597. ——: Idiopathic steatorrhea; identity of tropical and non-tropical sprue and intestinal infantilism, Arch. de mal de l'app. digestif 24:123, 1934.
598. ——: Idiopathic steatorrhea with special considerations of diognosis and occurrence of symptoms of endocrinopathy and avitaminosis: two cases, Hospitalstid. 77:1033, 1934.
599. ——: Idiopathic steatorrhea: ten cases, Quart. J. Med. 4:359, 1935.
600. ——: Idiopathic steatorrhea with particular emphasis on diagnosis and occurrence of symptoms of endocrinopathy and avitaminosis: two cases, Arch. f. Verdauungskr. 61:225, 1937.
601. Thaysen, T. E. H., and Norgaard, A.: Regulation of blood sugar in idiopathic steatorrhea (sprue and Gee-Herter's disease); low blood sugar curve, Arch. Int. Med. 44:17, 1929.
602. Tho, A.: Celiac disease, Nord. Med. 42:762, 1949.
603. Thompson, L.: Folic acid therapy in celiac disease, Brit. M. J. 1:297, 1948.
604. Thomson, J.: Two cases of infantilism, Tr. Med. Chir. Soc. Edinburgh 23:165, 1903-1904.
605. Thomson, M. L., et al.: Megaloblastic anemia in celiac disease treated with folic acid, Lancet 2:238, 1949.
606. Thursfield, H.: Case with unusual features, Proc. Roy. Soc. Med. 28:154, 1934.
607. Tisdall, F. F., et al.: Carbohydrate metabolism of the normal infant, Am. J. Dis. Child. 30:675, 1925.
608. Tislowitz, R.: Vitamin B_1 and carbohydrate metabolism, Klin. Wchnschr. 16:226, 1937.
609. Tobler, L.: Concerning pseudo-ascites as a result of chronic enteritis, Deutsch. Arch. f. klin. Med. 80:288, 1904.
610. Torrey, J. C.: Effect of lactose and dextrose on intestinal flora, J. Infect. Dis. 16:72, 1915.
611. Tuck, I. M., and Whittaker, N.: Vitamin B12 in idiopathic steatorrhea (with megaloblastic anemia), Lancet 1:757, 1950.
612. Tudor, R. B., and Platou, E. S.: Celiac disease, J. Lancet 66:142, 1946.
613. Tverdy, G., and Froelich, A. L.: Avitaminosis E during non-tropical sprue; case, Lille chir. 4:109, 1949.
614. Valdes y Carlos, J. M., and Piantoni, C.: Contribution to the treatment of celiac disease, Rev. méd. de Cordoba, 21:137, 1933.
615. Valette, G.: The mode of action of the anthroquinone purgatives, Compt. rend. Soc. de biol. 141:29, 1947.
616. Vallery-Radot, P.: Case in small child, Bull. Soc. de pédiat. de Paris 30:537, 1932.

617. Van Creveld, S.: Differentiation of pancreatogenic fatty stool in children, Nederl. tijdschr. v. geneesk. 76:3741, 1932.

618. Van Lohuizen, C. H. J.: Herter's infantilism; case, Nederl. tijdschr. v. Geneesk. 2:1896, 1927.

619. Vaughan, J. M.: Idiopathic steatorrhea, Internat. Clin. 4:18, 1935.

620. Vaughan, J. M., and Hunter, V.: Treatment by marmite (yeast extract) of megalocytic hyperchromic anemia occurring in idiopathic steatorrhea (celiac disease), Lancet 1:829, 1932.

621. Veghelyi, P. C. D.: Imitated by giardiasis, Am. J. Dis. Child. 57:894, 1939.

622. Velasco Blanco, L.: Diagnosis, pathogenesis, and therapy; case, Arch. am. de med. 8:125, 1932.

623. ——: Etiology, Arch. am. de med. 15:1, 1939.

624. Velasco Blanco, L., et al.: Celiac disease and avitaminosis: case, Arch. am. de med. 12:29, 1936.

625. Verzar, F.: Adrenal cortex and intestinal absorption, Am. J. Digest. Dis. and Nutrition 4:545, 1937.

626. Verzar, F., and McDougall, E. J.: Absorption from the Intestine, London, Longmans, 1936.

627. Vipond, A. E.: Banana flour and plantain meal as a food for children suffering from diarrhea, Montreal M. J. 39:590, 1910.

628. ——: Diarrhea in children with especial reference to dividivi as a drug, to banana flour and plantain meal as a food, Arch. Pediat. 28:244, 1911.

629. ——: Further observations upon banana flour as a food for infants, Am. Med. 21:450, 1926.

630. Vogt, J. H., and Tønsager, A.: Bone chemistry of man: experiments to determine phosphatase, nitrogen, phosphorus, and cancer in spongy iliac crest after vitamin D2 medication in steatorrhea and in Cushing's syndrome, Acta med. scandinav. 135:245, 1949.

631. Vogtmøller, P., and Lawaetz, B.: Studies on serviceability of hemolipocrit method and on course of alimentary hyperlipemia in patients suffering from idiopathic steatorrhea, Acta med. scandinav. 92:105, 1937.

632. Von Den Steinen, R.: Treatment of Heubner-Herter's disease with bananas, sour milk, and junket, Arch. f. Kinederh. 84:144, 1928.

633. Von Meysenburg, L.: Experiences with banana feeding in infants, Arch. Pediat. 45:509, 1928.

634. ——: The role of banana in the diet of infants, New Orleans M. & S. J. 82:74, 1929.

635. Von Meysenburg, L., and Fine, A.: Banana powder and the fecal flora of infants, J. Pediat. 8:630, 1936.

636. Von Reuss, A.: The significance of carbohydrates in digestive disturbances of children, Bibl. z. d. Mitt. d. Ges. f. inn. Med. u. Kinderh. in Wien 9:101, 1910.
637. Wade, A. E.: Intestinal absorption and gastro-intestinal motility, J. Pediat. 8:563, 1936.
638. Wall, J. S.: Ccliac disease, Internat. Clin. 1:255, 1938.
639. Wampler, F. J., and Forbes, J. C.: Calcium and phosphorus metabolism in case, South. M. J. 26:555, 1933.
640. ——: Celiac disease with osteomalacia-like bone changes, Virginia M. Monthly 61:11, 1934.
641. Warner, E. C.: Tuberculosis peritonitis simulating celiac disease, Brit. M. J. 1:977, 1931.
642. Webster, J., and Perkins, H.: Celiac infantilism; its fat digestion and treatment by bile salts, Lancet 2:894, 1920.
643. Weinstein, L., and Weiss, J. E.: Influence of certain dried fruits and adsorbing agents on intestinal flora of white mice, J. Infect. Dis. 60:128, 1937.
644. Weir, J. F., and Adams, M.: Idiopathic steatorrhea; metabolic studies during treatment: case, Proc. Staff Meet. Mayo Clin. 9:743, 1934.
645. ——: Idiopathic steatorrhea: metabolic study of patient, with reference to utilization of nitrogen and fat, Arch. Int. Med. 56:1109, 1935.
646. Wendt, H.: Chronic intestinal disturbances with decalcification of bones in adult; relation to celiac disease in children, Med. Klin. 30:187, 1934.
647. Wernstedt, W.: A case of infantilism? Acta paediat. 15:131, 1933-1934.
648. West, C. D., et al.: Blood amino nitrogen levels, Am. J. Dis. Child. 72:251, 1946.
649. Wigglesworth, F. W.: Fibrocystic disease of the pancreas, Am. J. Med. Sci. 212:351, 1946.
650. Williams, C. T.: Diagnosis and treatment with report of two cases, New Orleans M. & S. J. 81:642, 1929.
651. Wolfstein, S.: Case of Herter-Heubner's disease, Warsz. czas. lěk. 12:443, 1935.
652. Wollarger, E., et al.: Efficiency of the gastro-intestinal tract after resection of the head of the pancreas, J. A. M. A. 137:838, 1948.
653. Woltman, H. W., and Heck, F. J.: Funicular degeneration of spinal cord without pernicious anemia: neurologic aspects of sprue, non-tropical sprue, and idiopathic steatorrhea, Arch. Int. Med. 60:272, 1937.
654. Woringer, P.: Celiac disease, J. méd. Paris 50:721, 1930.
655. Yampolsky, Y.: Use of banana diet in treatment of chronic intestinal indigestion in children, J. M. A. Georgia 16:302, 1927.

656. Zellweger, H., and Lauchli, P.: Herter's infantilism and sprue: catamnestic studies on 22 patients, Helvet. paediat. acta 5:330, 1950.
657. Zingg, W.: Severe diverticulosis of jejunum as partial cause of sprue syndrome, Gastroenterologia 75:353, 1949-1950.

ADDENDA

1. Dicke, W. K.: Celiac disease; investigation of the harmful effects of certain types of cereal on patients with celiac disease, Thesis, Utrecht, 1950.
2. Ehner, D.: Chronic intestinal indigestion in children, N. Y. State J. M. 23:192, 1923.
3. Feer, K.: Infantilism treated with pancreatic extract, Am. J. Dis. Child. 2:332, 1911.
4. Lapp, F. W., and Torriani, C. L.: Blood sugar curve after fractional fruit and white bread test, Med. Klin. 27:1635, 1931.
5. Lowe, C. U., and May, C. D.: Metabolic studies in patients with intolerance to complex carbohydrates, Am. J. Dis. Child. 81:81, 1951.
6. Marfan, A. B.: Disease of intestinal absorption, Nourisson 28:1, 1940.
7. Marriott, W. McK.: Celiac disease, Pediatrics 3:386, 1924.
8. Martinez, Vargas: Celiac disease, Med. ninos 36:326, 1935.
9. Mathieu, R., and Leroy, E.: Intestinal infantilism or Herter's disease, Arch. de mal. de l'app. digestif 22:834, 1932.
10. Mautner, H.: Celiac disease, Klin. Wchnschr. 4:164, 1925.
11. Potter, P. S.: Celiac disease, Arch. Pediat. 43:84, 1926.

Index